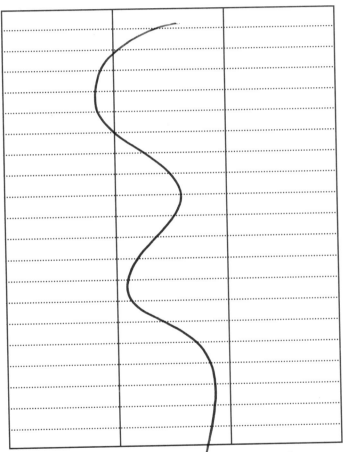

COUNTY LIBRARY

 Nottinghamshire County Council

Please return / renew by the
last date shown.

DP&P(O) 05.07/Comms/4261

Ted Hughes and Translation

Daniel Weissbort

·RICHARD HOLLIS·

First published in 2011
by Richard Hollis
an imprint of Five Leaves Publications
PO Box 8786
Nottingham NG1 9AW
info@fiveleaves.co.uk
www.fiveleaves.co.uk

ISBN: 978 1 907869 00 6

Designed and typeset by Richard Hollis

Printed by Short Run Press,
Exeter

Five Leaves acknowledges financial support
from Arts Council England

A CIP record for this book
is available from the
British Library

Contents

Introduction

However rootedly national in detail it may be, poetry is less and less the prisoner of its own language. It is beginning to represent, as an ambassador, something far greater than itself. Or perhaps it is only now being heard for what, among other things, it is – a universal language of understanding in which we can all hope to meet.[1]

Ted Hughes, introducing the first London Poetry International in 1967, was not speaking in a vacuum. After the devastations of World War II, mutual understanding between nations, separated historically as well as linguistically, assumed a new urgency. Among the less obvious indications was an increase in the number of multinational festivals, bringing artists of diverse cultures together in the hope or expectation of their finding ways of responding to one another, and encouraging mutual understanding.

Hughes's interest in the translation of poetry, however, predated Poetry International by several years. In 1964, with me, he founded the magazine *Modern Poetry in Translation (MPT)*; its first issue was published the following year. There was also a personal component, namely his involvement in translating poetry by two contemporaries, the Israeli poet Yehuda Amichai, examined here in Chapter 2, and the Hungarian János Pilinszky, in Chapter 3. I shall focus now, however, on Hughes's own writing, that is, on what may have disposed him to take an interest in translation in the first place.

Hughes sometimes mentioned the difficulty encountered in "getting started", experiencing a need to write so as to clear the "mental pathways". Although reluctance to commit anything to paper is not unusual, Ted Hughes's interest in writing by children is also related to his interest in the problem or difficulties of creativity, another aspect of this same concern being his commitment to the somewhat unfashionable discipline of memorization as well as to various austere intellectual skills. He drew certain conclusions from his experience of working with children, which involved him in visits to schools and, for instance, serving as a judge in a national children's writing competition sponsored by the *Daily Mirror*; he was also involved in an innovative series of radio programmes called "Listening and Writing".[2]

Translation is always an option. The work of writing – the hard part – has been done by the initial writer and the translator now arrives on the scene. Of course, he/she has a multitude of problems to solve, but these, however complex, are technical and, on the whole, readily enough dealt with. Naturally the source text is more than just a draft, or hardly worth agonizing over, although one approach to translating is precisely to treat it as a draft, to be rewritten, as it were, in another language.

Ted Hughes is commonly regarded as among the most "rooted" of English-language poets. At the same time he is seen as among the most internationally minded and ambitious, in that he reaches back into his own tradition (with its international connections, at a peak, during the Tudor period), as well as into the world about him. It was curiosity about contemporary non-English poetry that induced him to engage in translation. Intuitively, Hughes at first reckoned that the best approach was to be as literal as possible, and his introductory essays to his translations both of Yehuda Amichai's Hebrew poetry and of János Pilinzsky's characteristically Hungarian voice, display the conviction that non-intrusive or minimal translation will accomplish as much as may be hoped for. His primary concern was to familiarize an English poetry-reading public – and' he hoped, English poets – with work done elsewhere, especially, as it turned out, contemporary writing in what might be regarded as historically less fortunate parts of Europe.

It is perhaps facile to suggest that it was Hughes's very rootedness in the English tradition that disposed him to look beyond national or linguistic frontiers. In addition to being a highly gifted writer, he was also one of formidable intelligence, his occasional critical writings[3] and exploration of Shakespeare's plays being convincing evidence of this.[4] Much of Hughes's writing, in fact, had to do with an effort to promote certain practical or pedagogical objectives. Thus, *Poetry in the Making*, his anthology of poems from the radio series 'Listening and Writing', was directed at teachers of English literature and constituted an attempt to alert the teaching profession to the talent so often mutilated or at least unnurtured by the system. As Poet Laureate, he frequently visited schools, talking to students about poetry. It may fairly be said that he had accepted the official appointment primarily because he hoped it would provide him with political leverage, a platform from which to present his views, influencing educational and environmental policy (of which, more later), the downside being that elevation to the laureateship also inevitably exposed him even more to the attacks of unfriendly critics.

Hughes was convinced that the journal he helped to found, *Modern Poetry in Translation*, would help alter English poetic sensibility and wanted the magazine to be more generally available than is usual with such esoteric publications; at one time, as he wrote in an editorial, the idea was even toyed with of sending free copies to every poet in England. Hughes's selections from the works of Emily Dickinson and Keith Douglas,[5] with his introductory essays, also had a pedagogical purpose. Similarly, of course, his selection of verse from Shakespeare's plays, with an introduction foreshadowing his *Shakespeare and the Goddess of Complete Being*, shared his insights into what he saw as the bard's visionary design.[6] By temperament, Hughes, without aspiring so to be, was a teacher, with the professional awareness of the resistance to be expected and on the lookout for ways of overcoming it.

As regards the journal *MPT*, Hughes's enthusiasm and confidence were not always well taken. Translation, in itself of course, and more so in relation to poetry produced by poets of Eastern Europe a little older than himself – his attendance at poetry festivals had brought him into contact with these individuals – became an obsession. He persuaded the Arts Council of Great Britain, as it was then known, to support *MPT* and, via its Poetry Book Society, to underwrite his plans for an international poetry festival in London, inspired by the Spoleto Festival in Italy, at which he had met such poets as Miroslav Holub of Czechoslovakia and Zbigniew Herbert of Poland. One may speculate that, identifying with the less advantaged, his gaze was directed outwards. Hughes's rise to national and international prominence quickly placed certain possibilities within his grasp and he did not fail to make use of his growing prestige. He was a persuasive advocate and when he proposed the idea to me of a magazine devoted solely to foreign poetry in translation, I was at once energized by his vision. His advocacy of *MPT* and of Poetry International, his willingness to involve himself personally in the organization of the festival and detailed editing of the magazine, were due to his conviction and a clarity of vision, but also perhaps owed something to his marginal social status in what was still a class-bound society. That it was not due to familiarity with foreign languages or cultures seems certain – the only foreign languages with which Hughes had some familiarity were French – though even here he relied much on his sister Olwyn's knowledge – and Spanish, Spain being where he and Sylvia Plath had spent their honeymoon. He was, however, attuned to the needs and unusually sensitive to the tensions of a period following two World Wars.

Like his Renaissance predecessors, however, Hughes was drawn to foreign cultures, especially the ancient ones of Greece and Rome. Maybe it was his inherited insularity that, in part, stimulated his interest in translation, seen also, in its literal form, as a means of more direct contact with the *otherness* of the foreign original. He sought out and worked with individuals willing to provide him with literal versions or, as in the case of Amichai, with their own English versions of their writings, the English in question being non-conventional and eccentrically personal or provisional. As he put it in his editorial to *MPT 3*, with Yehuda Amichai in mind:

> *A man who has something really serious to say in a language of which he knows only a few words, manages to say it far more convincingly and effectively than any interpreter, and in translated poetry it is the first hand contact – however fumbled and broken – with that man and his seriousness which we want. The minute we gloss his words we have more or less what he said but we have lost him. We are ringing changes – amusing though they may be – on our own familiar abstractions, and are no longer reaching through to what we have not experienced before, which is alive and real.[7]*

This seemed almost to anticipate experiments with an invented language, "Orghast". In his reworking or revisions of the Amichai texts, Hughes made only what he felt were essential changes, convinced of the privileged status of the Israeli poet's own English versions, which he saw as Amichai's own English poems. His work, then, was an exercise in hands-off, rather than hands-on, translation; he altered nothing in Amichai's drafts for the sake of change or to impose his own imprint, intent only on removing obstructions by minimal re-wording or re-phrasing. Even there, he hesitated, aware that there might be something to be learnt from a foreign poet's apparent "abuse" of the target language.

Hughes, wishing to experience the source as immediately as possible and to convey this in English with as little overlay as possible from his (as he put it) personal "translation manual", may remind us of T. S. Eliot's comment on Gilbert Murray's versions of Greek drama: "Professor Murray has simply interposed between Euripides and ourselves a barrier more impenetrable than the Greek language".[8] Not concerned with displaying his literary skills, Hughes was intent on rendering a service to source texts of moment from which he was simultaneously learning. Much flows from this modest ambition, of course, not least having to do with poetic form, the reproduction of which is often incompatible with literalism.

It seems that Hughes was reaching out, much as his Renaissance predecessors had done (for example, Arthur Golding, translator of Ovid's *Metamorphoses*, see Chapter V). This is particularly important, after the First and Second World Wars and following a period in which England, in spite of its imperial pretensions and continuing worldwide responsibilities, was cut off even from its immediate European neighbours and had turned in on itself. With the end of the Second World War, Europe, of course, was divided by an "iron curtain", in that the other side continued to remind us of its existence, but an impenetrable barrier had been erected between us and it. For some years, it seemed likely that ideological differences, and the ambitions of the Soviet Union, might provoke another war, a virtually unthinkable prospect, due to the development of weapons of mass-destruction. And yet human beings were not simply ideologically definable, but shared concerns and interests, even beyond the overriding one of survival of the species.

As the Soviet system began to disintegrate, observers became aware of the key role played by apparently powerless artists and writers, especially writers such as Vaclav Havel, the Czech President and himself a celebrated avant-garde playwright, who wrote an important essay on this very theme, entitled "The Power of the Powerless".[9] Hughes, given his obsession with war (especially that of his father's, the so-called Great War), and his interest in historical developments, and also due to his status as a leading poet, was particularly aware of this, and was routinely invited to literary festivals where he met the new proponents of human dignity and individuality in Eastern Europe, mostly born in the 1920s, belonging to the older-brother generation. His Introduction to *Modern Poetry in Translation* (1982) describes the reasons for a boom in the translation of poetry in what looked alarmingly like an *entre-deux-guerres* period.[10]

Possessing marked powers of concentration, Hughes, as noted, also expressed a belief in the value of memorization, as a mental discipline and way of internalizing the work of another writer. He went so far as to proselytize these seemingly old-fashioned views, but also took an interest in "mind maps", an aid to memorization developed in the late 1960s by the author and broadcaster Tony Buzan, and was drawn to various meditation techniques. Hughes was open-minded when it came to investigating and experimenting with so-called occult disciplines, such as Kabbala and astrology, and also investigated neo-Platonism, and such beliefs as those of the Rosicrucians, impressed in particular by the writings of Frances Yates on this aspect of Renaissance intellectual life.[11]

11

For Hughes, translation of poetry was another such technique or discipline, a means of drawing closer to admired writers, of focusing his ability to listen, *to hear*. Evidently, he regarded it as his duty to place himself at the disposal of these writers, assisting their work to cross language frontiers. He discovered, probably not to his surprise, that those seeking less mediated contact with source texts were not well catered for, though the field of literary translation was a relatively well-cultivated one, with poets often more eager to display familiar talents than to convey something that, at first, seemed merely outlandish.

From the start, Hughes did his best not to substitute himself for the source-text author. He was occasionally criticized on this account, notably in connection with his versions of János Pilinszky's poetry, where his American publisher, on advice from a source-language consultant, turned down the translation as being too constricted by the literalistic renderings of his co-translators. For Hughes, however, as suggested, translation was an exercise in close or attentive listening, rather than an opportunity to display his literary talents. What enabled him to assimilate the foreign material was precisely that he stayed focused on the source, not just its content but even on the texture of the language, insofar as this could be apprehended. With Amichai, the source-language poet's bilingualism was the bridge, Amichai possessing fluent if idiosyncratic English and having been influenced by English poetry, especially that of Auden. In the case of János Pilinszky, Hughes was able to make contact on a personal level via French, Pilinszky's second language, as well by the English versions of an intimate of both author and translator, János Csokits, the distinguished émigré Hungarian poet, contemporary of Pilinszky and friend of Hughes's Paris-based sister, Olwyn.

Where he had no live collaborators, as in his translation of classical texts, Hughes drew on literalistic or scholarly renderings, available, for instance, in the Loeb Classical Library editions, and also read as many versions as he could find (e.g., William Arrowsmith's translation of Euripides' *Alcestis*). Hughes's vision or understanding was bound to be partial, but he never claimed that his versions were for all time, and indeed no translation, however admirable, however much even it becomes a fixture in the literature of the target language, remains a permanent or final authoritative rendering, this being true even of so hugely influential a work as the seventeenth-century Authorised Version of the Bible, the cadences of which have been integrated into English. Hughes was aware of this and is quoted in relation to Everett Fox's translation of the Pentateuch: "For once, since the King James, a translation that comes right out of the heart of the living culture of the thing. I read it with real excitement, like a wholly new real text." [12]

One feels constrained to explain or justify the interest of so distinctly English a writer not just in the promotion of translation, but in its business and politics, even though until comparatively recently translation was routinely practised by such celebrated writers as Pope, Dryden or Ezra Pound, translations, in fact, forming the bulk of their work.

Although this is not the place for a history of translation, it is permissible to quote Pound who, in his essay on Tudor translators, remarks: "A great age of literature is perhaps always a great age of translation, or follows it." [13] Pound, incidentally, influenced translation in our time well beyond his own translations of Provençal, Anglo-Saxon and classical Chinese poetry. Hughes, like others who took an interest in translation in the 1950s, was not immune to his example. He wrote apropos of his own translations of Amichai:

> *What I wanted to preserve above all was the tone and cadence of Amichai's own voice speaking in English which seems to me marvellously true to the poetry, in these renderings. What Pound called the first of all poetic virtues – 'the heart's tone'. So, as translations these are extremely literal. But they are also more, they are Yehuda Amichai's own English poems.* [14]

Hughes seems to be positing the achievability of identity between source and target texts. This idealistic view may originate in the special status of English at this time, its use, diplomatically and professionally, certainly as regards the sciences. Perhaps, not surprisingly, a writer of the reach and ambition of Hughes was drawn to dreams of linguistic universalism, which has a religious dimension, insofar as the great religions aspire to traverse linguistic and cultural divides. Nevertheless, the last thing to which Hughes aspired was to legislate for others.

The East European poets who concerned Hughes and myself when we began *MPT* (especially Tadeusz Rózewicz, Vasko Popa, Miroslav Holub and Zbigniew Herbert) had been impelled by historical experience to create or improvise what appeared to be new. The cause of "literalism", thus, was espoused, but it was not really taken into account that this was far from a straightforward or uncontroversial position, and that absolute literalism was, in any case, a logical impossibility, no two languages being substitutable for one another. Literalism, however, seemed to be that to which the "new" poetry aspired, so that the literal translation into the target-language

English, the twentieth-century's *lingua franca*, apparently lay, like a shadowy presence, between the text in the source-language and the target text or translation into a second language, constituting a means of linguistic transferability.

This, of course, was more a matter of faith than of intellectual conviction, given the problems of translating poetry in the first place, and poetry being identifiable with the language in which it is composed. Thus sound, so essential a component of the means by which a poem functions, could not be repeated or even imitated. Literal translation being a manifest contradiction in terms, what poetry seems to require of its translator is re-creation. Hughes, however, felt that at least some of the poetry being written in the postwar period could, in fact, be reproduced in literal fashion, itself being written in a language that effectively transcended language, so that what was needed was not the re-creative zeal or overdrive of the translating poet but, rather surprisingly, the modest literalist ambitions of the scribe, assisted, ideally, by the source poet. It seemed to Hughes that the poetry of, say, János Pilinszky, had been written under such pressure that it was a new thing, virtually dictating its translation into English:

> The sense of selfless, courageous testimony pushed to a near-saintly pitch is very strong in Pilinszky. It puts a translator under exacting obligations to remain as close to the actual Hungarian wording as possible and interdicting recourse to the translator's personal resources anything from the translator's own poetical medicine bag.[15]

Hughes, a poet with an exceptionally well-stocked "medicine bag" of his own, was eager to be of service in this respect and the contribution of so talented a writer was, in fact, what was needed. This may seem paradoxical, but a closer examination of actual translation projects undertaken by Hughes should make the meaning clearer. It must also be borne in mind that Hughes was unusually attentive to foreign poetry, in literal translations, and seemed able to reconstruct something like an original on the basis of these texts. His collaborator, János Csokits, commented on this ability:

> It is almost as if he could X-ray the literals and see the original poem in ghostly detail like a radiologist viewing the bones, muscles, veins and nerves of a live human body. The difference is that X-ray pictures do not show the human face, whereas Hughes can see and visualise the whole astral body of the poem. It is eerie when this happens; one can almost hear the humming of a high tension line, but the effect is not that of a technical device; it has more to do with extra-sensory perception.[16]

I

Modern Poetry in Translation

Ted Hughes's interest in translating poetry and, in general, in poetry translated into English, predates his plans for a magazine which became *Modern Poetry in Translation* (*MPT*). As is shown by his correspondence with Sonia Raiziss, the founder-editor of the New York literary journal *Chelsea*, Hughes conceived the idea of a publication devoted exclusively to modern poetry in English translation while he was living in America. He received encouragement from American friends and returned to England persuaded that this novel idea was also a timely one, not unlikely to engage the interest of the English literary world, making it also a practical proposition.

Hughes and I had met as undergraduates at Cambridge and he first broached the notion of a magazine to me at a New Year's Party, 1962 to 1963, in London, not long after his return and shortly before Sylvia Plath's death. It took about two years for *MPT* to be launched, but we began almost at once to investigate the foreign scene, as it were, and the prospects for such an initiative. Fairly soon I came across two outstanding poets, hardly, if at all, translated into English: the Israeli Yehuda Amichai and the Yugoslav (Serbian) Vasko Popa. In addition, I was introduced to the names of a number of other poets, mostly from Eastern and Central Europe and from the Soviet Union, the latter country being in my own field of study, as I was a graduate student at the London School of Economics, investigating literature in the Soviet Union during the period of de-Stalinization.

Some of the poets who caught our attention – for instance, the Czech poet and immunologist Miroslav Holub – Hughes had also encountered at the Spoleto International Poetry Festival (*Festival dei due Mondi*) where the public was supplied with unpretentious English versions. It was these versions that Hughes brought back with him. They had been intended to facilitate listening to the foreign poetry but also inspired Hughes with the idea that a magazine featuring unpretentious translations of this sort was a viable project. The barriers between Eastern and Western Europe, at least, were relatively permeable in the period following Stalin's death in 1953, and Hughes was drawn to the postwar East European poets of the generation immediately preceding his own, who had lived and were still living in oppressive, albeit changing circumstances. As he put it, these circumstances had "brought their poetry down to such precisions, discriminations and humilities that it is a new thing".[1] It was his perception of the "newness"of this poetry, unusually accessible, it seemed, even in literal translation, that persuaded him that the time was ripe for a journal, the main business of which would be to showcase such work in English translation.

Hughes and I co-edited *MPT* for ten issues, until 1971, after which Hughes withdrew from the editorship but continued to take an interest in the journal, which became a magnet for translated poetry, being for a while unique in the English-speaking world. *MPT* also helped to bring a number of poets to Hughes's closer attention, notably the Israeli Yehuda Amichai, but also the aforementioned Serbian poet Vasko Popa and the Hungarian János Pilinszky. Work by the first and last of these Hughes himself translated, and Popa's poetry he did much to promote, since it already had a dedicated translator in Anne Pennington.

The magazine was boosted not only because it was an intriguingly novel venture, but also because Hughes himself promoted it so vigorously. It received the support of the Arts Council of Great Britain, which also adopted Hughes's idea for an international poetry festival, still known as Poetry International. The first of these gatherings took place in 1967, directed by Ted Hughes and Patrick Garland, with Hughes himself and the actor Patrick Wymark reading the translations. These international readings helped widen the horizon of the poetry public in England, not only introducing hitherto unfamiliar non-English-language poets, but even major Americans, such as John Berryman, Charles Olson, Anne Sexton, Anthony Hecht, and Allen Ginsberg, as unfamiliar at that time, at least to most of the literary public as, for instance, Yehuda Amichai, Yves Bonnefoy and Hans Magnus Enzensberger. Although the *weltanschauung* was indeed propitious, Hughes's role was essential. He realized that it was not enough to espouse a likely cause, but also necessary to get it adopted by influential people.

Hughes wrote elliptically about his translation work, but did contribute a fairly straightforward piece on collaborative translation, the co-translation with his friend János Csokits of a selection of poetry by János Pilinszky.[2] In a collection of texts I assembled by translators of poetry, Hughes claimed that faithfulness to the literal version of the original is what is required but only rarely provided.[3] With Pilinszky, he said, he regarded himself "as the 'troubled mechanic' rather than Csokits's 'co-pilot'", concluding: "I am certain I would never have become as interested in Pilinszky as I eventually did, if my curiosity had not been caught in the first place by Csokits' swift word-for-word translations from the page at odd times during our long friendship."[4] He continues: "But even more exciting, for me, was the knack he had of projecting a raw, fresh sense of the strange original – the particular and to me alien uniqueness of the original."

In his sketch of what particularly drew him to this poetry, Hughes alludes to an earlier obsession of his with war itself, originating in his relationship with his father, a survivor of the Gallipoli campaign of the First World War: "[T]here emerges ... a strange creature, a gasping, limbless trunk, saved by primal hunger, among the odds and ends of a destroyed culture, waiting to be shot, or beaten to death, or just thrown on a refuse heap – or simply waiting in empty eternity."[5] Later, he acknowledges that "It is impossible not to feel that the spirit of his poetry aspires to the most naked and helpless of all confrontations, a Christ-like posture of crucifixion. His silence is the silence of that moment on the cross, after the cry." Pilinszky himself once remarked: "I would like to write as if I had remained silent."[6] Silence, wordlessness, the inability of language to match the war horrors, had, it seems, driven Hughes as well to search for a language relating to religion, so that his writing on translation sometimes appears quasi-religious. It is no surprise that Hughes observed of Pilinszky's poetry, that it put a translator "under exacting obligations" and that there was no question of introducing anything "from the translator's own poetical medicine bag".

The earliest issues of *MPT* subscribed to what might be described as a literalistic view. If Hughes was, perhaps, one of very few major translators to adhere to this, it was not so much because he was reluctant to receive credit for his work, as that the obligations seemed so pressing. *MPT*, under his direction, was almost notorious for its promotion of a severe viewpoint, unfashionable then and still so.

Concerned that credit should be given where he felt it was due, Hughes initially had wanted to include in his Introduction to the selection of Pilinszky's poetry, Csokits's literal and annotated version of one of the major poems, "Requiem". He decided, however, that his versions inched "so close to his [Csokits's] that there would be no point now in printing two almost identical texts".[7] Earlier, with regard to his translations of the Israeli poet Amichai, Hughes had similarly insisted that what he wanted to do was to "preserve above all [...] the tone and cadence of Amichai's own voice speaking in English, which seems to me marvellously true to the poetry..."[8] Himself so attuned to the virtues of this course, he was optimistically convinced that others would be as well. Amichai had supplied Hughes with English versions, which Hughes, true to his intention, revised minimally. Hughes and Amichai met in person occasionally and corresponded, but according to Amichai's widow their consultations were often by telephone. In 1970, Ted Hughes had written to Amichai, apropos the Penguin selection of the latter's poetry: "When I read your poems I get the feeling poems are waiting everywhere and ready to be made out of anything – wonderful sense of richness and abundance. There are just a few places where the English is obscure or too roundabout. I'll go through it in detail and send you a list of my queries."[9] Hughes was convinced that Amichai's inventiveness, his abundance of inspiration and naturalness of expression must not be overlaid by his English translator's literary mannerisms, of which, at that time and at all times, he was, in any case, suspicious. So keenly was Hughes able to sense what demanded a hearing that he felt a need to lend it his energy and time, however pressing other demands might be, especially those of his more immediate work.

Hughes's involvement in translation, in fact, is consistent with his sense of responsibility to poetry in the largest sense. Arguably, this was the product not only of his expansive vision, but was also encouraged by the times, including Hughes's indirect experience of war, another factor being his awareness of the dire politico-ecological crisis facing humanity in general and Western humanity in particular. At about this time, Hughes allowed his name to be used in the founding of an environmental magazine, *Your Environment* (1969), edited by a Cambridge contemporary, the children's writer and poet David Ross. The threat to the environment was agonizingly evident to Hughes, primarily a poet of nature. He was pessimistic about prospects, but this energized rather than paralyzed him, so that he continued to do what could be done and to look for means of expanding his influence. While his literary influence was used for the institution of an international poetry festival, he simultaneously attempted to draw attention to the environmental threat, a threat more immediate, more potentially catastrophic even than the danger of global military conflict.

Poets may be "unacknowledged legislators", but in Eastern Europe they were now officially so acknowledged, provided they toed the line. Hughes was concerned that this role should be taken more seriously and not just used as an excuse for having a good time or claiming a privileged status. With his friend, the children's writer Michael Morpurgo, he conceived the idea of a children's laureateship and sought to promote certain pedagogic aims through the Arvon Foundation, an educational trust with which he was closely associated, as well as through visits to schools and his connection to the *Daily Mirror*'s Children's Literary Competition. He also tried to encourage an awareness of the threat to the environment. Any of these concerns, and certainly all taken together, suggest a disposition which merits further discussion. Hughes's interest in translation, too, should be viewed in a global rather than narrowly national literary context.

The path envisaged by Hughes was not an easy one to follow and required a disciplined methodology. On the poetry of Amichai, for instance, Hughes initially collaborated with his friend Assia Gutmann, who had been brought up in Israel and had a knowledge of Hebrew. Later, he worked closely with the poet himself. His translations of Amichai's poetry, after Gutmann's death in 1969, were based mainly on Amichai's own English versions. Hughes insisted: "All I did was correct the more intrusive oddities and errors of grammar and usage, and in some places shift about the phrasing and line endings..."[10] He saw no virtue in intervention for its own sake, or in aligning the translated poetry with his own oeuvre, even if the final translations inevitably bear the imprint of his way with words.

Important also is what Hughes thought he was doing, even if his translation work is identifiably his own, as was that of predecessors, like Pope or Dryden their own. He was temperamentally disinclined to use other poets as a springboard for his own inventions, or to exploit their poetry as a filler in creatively lean times. Translating and promoting translation (e.g., the translations by Anne Pennington of Vasko Popa), he learned much that he was later able to use in his own work, *Crow* surely owing more than a little to Popa's example, Hughes and Popa sharing an interest in ethnology and folk imagination. Hughes's expertise was fostered by his studies at Cambridge, Popa's springing from his involvement in the development of Serbian national self-awareness.

I am also reminded of the editorial of the first issue of *Modern Poetry in Translation* (1965). Hughes's idea for the journal was persuasive, though it left many unpersuaded, even disgruntled, the *Times Literary Supplement*, for instance, dismissing the magazine as "at least a novelty". The editorial attempts to describe what we were after, at a time when there was no conventional language for such challenging notions:

> *The type of translations we are seeking can be described as literal,*
> *though not literal in a strict or pedantic sense. Though this may seem*
> *at first suspect, it is more apposite to define our criteria negatively as*
> *literalness can only be a deliberate tendency, not a dogma.*

All this was as least a decade before post-colonial translation theory had advanced the notion of "foreignization", as against the traditional approach of "domestication"; indeed, had the magazine begun somewhat later, it might have been welcomed, at least in some quarters, as another manifestation of the "post-colonial spirit". In the first chapter of a groundbreaking book by the American translation theorist and translator (from the Italian) Lawrence Venuti, the author warns against the much-touted quality of "Invisibility": "it doesn't read like a translation".[11] Hughes had questioned this from the start. As a Cambridge undergraduate, in 1955, he had come across a collection of folklore, compiled by the anthropologist W.H.I. Bleek.[12] In a *Modern Poetry in Translation Yearbook* editorial he refers to this, restating his devotion to literal translation, the propagation of which he saw as being the principal pedagogical purpose of *MPT*:

> *Since our only real motive in publishing was our own curiosity in con-*
> *temporary foreign poetry, we favoured the translations that best*
> *revealed the individuality and strangeness of the original. This usu-*
> *ally meant a translation that interposed the minimum of the reflexes*
> *and inventions of the translator. … But the most literal covers a wide*
> *range between denotative and connotative extremes. Ideally, we would*
> *have liked to see at least some poems translated with the concern for*
> *both extremes served as meticulously and flexibly as in Bleek's trans-*
> *lation of Bushman lore – though we understood the limited appeal of*
> *anything so raw and strange unless it has the guarantee behind it of a*
> *literary personality as solid, say, as Beckett's...*[13]

He realized that the nature of this challenge to received opinion regarding literary translation and especially translation of poetry was a radical one. In an editorial to *MPT* 3 (Spring 1967), he turned to the kind of translation he had in mind, exemplified by Yehuda Amichai's English versions of his own Hebrew poems. Then he warned: "The minute we gloss his words, we have more or less what he said but we have lost him. We are ringing changes [...] on our own familiar abstractions and are no longer reaching through to what we have not experienced before, which is alive and real." This warning now seems more problematical, especially with regard to the assumption about the possibility of communication across language frontiers, and conveys an optimistic view of the potential for mutual understanding that not all will associate with Ted Hughes, so often seen as a poet of the dark side.

The English language is now far from being a unitary linguistic phenomenon; it is indeed a *lingua franca*, as Latin, in its more limited geographical context, had been. The "Queen's English", the language of the English upper- and educated middle-classes, is no longer the dominant form. Hughes's own English owed at least as much to Yorkshire usage as it did to standard, educated English, based on the Germanized English of the Victorian court. He could scarcely have been unaware that what he was proposing, was radical, that is, that Bleek's anthropological translations of Bushman lore might serve as a model for translation of poetry in general. Even a decade or so after post-colonial translation theorists have commended "foreignization", in an era when "political correctness" seems to have legitimized such a strategy, Hughes's approach may seem idealistic or impractical. When his American publisher rejected his Pilinszky translations (first published in the UK in 1976 by Carcanet), Hughes wrote to me acidly:

> He [the Hungarian consultant] said he just could not see anything in my translations. Says I'd let myself be strait-jacketed by my co-translator, tied up in literal word for word renderings of the Hungarian inspirations. Where were Pilinszky's exciting rhythms? None of my versions 'takes off from the literal.

Hughes was clearly disappointed that his publishers had not seen or did not agree with the rationale for his cautiously advocated approach, which he had tried to define in his introductory essay. Hughes's appeal had apparently fallen on deaf ears, and what the Hungarian consultant wanted, as a representative of a language of "limited diffusion", was more attractive to the publisher. Wrongly, in Hughes's view, it was assumed that the desired transformation could occur only if the translator was inspired and free, unconstrained by his source.

At this point, the comments of a distinguished interpreter of South Indian sacred poetry, A.K. Ramanujan, seem apposite. Hughes greatly admired Ramanujan's *Speaking of Siva*.[14] In a letter to me from America about *Gaudete* (1977), alluding to the series of poems in the Epilogue to that book, supposedly composed by Rev. Lumb himself, Hughes explained:

> I once wrote a film scenario about a priest who turns all the women of his parish into his coven ... I just re-wrote it, much altered, in a sort of verse, very crude lead-pipe verse ... He gets killed at the end but then resurrects and writes a lot of poems which I quite like. They started

being vacanas — as in that Speaking of Shiva book — but then took off on their own.

In his Translator's Note, Ramanujan had written: "In the act of translating, 'the Spirit killeth and the letter giveth Life'." This literalist approach was to Hughes's liking and seemed to underwrite contentions such as those of the anthropologist Bleek. The English language, Hughes felt, was now particularly responsive to such attempts to use it as a means of conveying the "foreignness" of non-English source texts.

One should also invoke the work of Walter Benjamin, in particular his essay "The Task of the Translator", an introduction to his own translation of Baudelaire's poetry.[15] This was an essay that Hughes read, as it appeared in 1968 in the second issue of the translation journal *Delos*, edited by Keith Botsford, himself a translator of Latin-American poetry. Benjamin's essay cannot easily be summarized and I shall quote only its conclusion: "For to some degree all great texts contain their virtual translation between the lines. This is true to the highest degree of sacred writings. The interlinear version of the Scriptures is the prototype or ideal of all translation." Martin Buber and Franz Rosenzweig, German-language translators of the Bible, drawing on Benjamin's work, provided the theoretical and practical basis for the rabbinically trained Everett Fox's Bible translation.[16] In a 1926 lecture, Buber urges readers to "ponder aloud the words written in the book in front of you; hear the word you utter and let it reach you."

Hughes's suspicion of translations that aimed to replace the source texts with naturalized English ones was not well-received. There continues to be much scepticism about the claim that the words of the source text are the key, that what is required is attention to these rather than to the translator's own re-creative zeal, the Ciceronian tradition of sense-for-sense rather than word-for-word having prevailed at least since the Tudor period, and confidence in it only recently having declined to the point where "foreignization", or close attention to the actual wording of the source-text, and even to the syntax, has been considered a viable alternative.

From Hughes's point of view, it is Vladimir Nabokov, perhaps, who uttered the last word on this topic. Nabokov, in his version of Pushkin's *Eugene Onegin* practised a deliberate form of literalism.

The scholar will be, I hope, exact and pedantic: footnotes – on the same page as the text and not tucked away at the end of the volume – can never be too copious and detailed. ... [T]he point is ... that ... both ... are hopelessly devoid of any semblance of creative genius. ... Now comes

> *the authentic poet who has the two last assets and who finds relaxation in translating a bit of Lermontov or Verlaine between writing poems of his own. ... The main drawback, however, in this case is the fact that the greater his individual talent, the more apt he will be to drown the foreign masterpiece under the sparkling ripples of his own personal style. Instead of dressing up like the real author, he dresses up the author as himself.[17]*

In the case of his own translation of Lermontov's *A Hero of Our Time* (1958) Nabokov ironized:

> *This is the first English translation of Lermontov's novel. The book has been paraphrased into English several times, but never translated before. The experienced hack may find it quite easy to turn Lermontov's Russian into slick English clichés by means of judicious omission, amplification, and levitation; and he will tone down everything that might seem unfamiliar to the meek and imbecile reader visualized by his publisher. But the honest translator is faced with a different task.[18]*

And his famously scornful characterization of previous attempts to translate *Onegin* reads:

> *What is translation? On a platter*
> *A poet's pale and glaring head,*
> *A parrot's screech, a monkey's chatter,*
> *And profanation of the dead.[19]*

Though his ironical humour might not commend itself in our politer times, in Part IV of his essay "Problems of Translation: 'Onegin' in English", he effectively outlines the problems. His view that only "literal' translation, admittedly as defined and characterized by himself, deserves the name of translation is synthesized as follows:

> *The person who desires to turn a literary masterpiece into another language, has only one duty to perform, and this is to reproduce with absolute exactitude the whole text, and nothing but the text. The term "literal translation" is tautological since anything but that is not truly a translation but an imitation, an adaptation or a parody. [...] [S]horn of its primary verbal existence, the original text will not be able to soar and to sing; but it can be very nicely dissected and mounted, and scientifically studied in all its organic details.[20]*

I have quoted Nabokov because Hughes took so many hints from him even if he could not aspire to such scholarly exactitude. Hughes admired the

Russian author's controversial translation of *Onegin* and insisted that this was the only English version that gave him any sense of the claimed greatness of the source text, of Pushkin himself, a poet in whose work Hughes was greatly interested; note also that one of his own last poems was the translation of a poem by Pushkin, "*Prorok*/The Prophet". But Nabokov's view has few supporters, even among Slavists, browbeaten into supporting the egocentric position of the poet-translators.

In his Introduction to his translation of and commentary on Pushkin's novel-in-verse, Nabokov boasted:

> *In transposing Eugene Onegin from Pushkin's Russian into my English I have sacrificed to completeness of meaning every formal element ... (elegance, euphony, clarity, good taste, modern usage, and even grammar) that the dainty mimic prizes higher than truth. ...*

Hughes subscribed to this modest ambition, contributing a brief introduction to the official programme of the first Poetry International in London (1967), a blurb for what, in England, was a pioneering enterprise, but which also suggests a certain familiarity with the issues involved, recalling, in more familiar terms, what Walter Benjamin had written about an ur-text or original language, underlying both source and target texts, to which both refer, a metaphysical notion and one which appeared to resonate for Hughes as well.

In espousing the cause of a "higher literalism", Hughes, was challenging not only the emphasis on individualism, the primacy of the individual voice of the translator-poet, but a tradition of "domestication", making the poem accessible in everyday language. His was an austere viewpoint, which predated somewhat his interest in translation that attempted to represent the source work in its uniqueness, and which assumed that the translator's task was to make explicit this connection, not superimpose a new text, while he pleaded that this was the best that could be hoped for. The dream of achieving identity is unrealistic, but it was held by Hughes and others, Ramanujan being among them, that in accepting its impossibility, translation had drifted too far, opening the gates to what Dryden somewhat dismissively called "imitation". Imitation, on the other hand, seems a legitimate literary form and strategy and surely one of the ways that texts are enabled to travel between literary cultures. But Dryden's caveat, in the Preface to Ovid's *Epistles* (1680) should still be borne in mind:

> *The third way is that of imitation, where the translator (if now he has not lost that name) assumes the liberty not only to vary from the words and sense, but to forsake them both as he sees occasion, and taking only*

*some general hints from the original, to run division on the ground-
work as he pleases.*

Like Dryden, Hughes believed that something closer than this was achievable. He once collected Goethe's memorable sayings, the latter maintaining that only he who had translated into it could be said to know his own language. Hughes might surely have also specified that for this to happen the translator must pay close attention to the wording and syntax of the source-text.

II
Yehuda Amichai
The Authenticity of Self-Translation

Yehuda Amichai (1924-2000) was born in Würzburg, Germany, into an orthodox, Hebrew-speaking Jewish family, and emigrated to Palestine in 1936. He served in the Jewish Brigade of the British Army during World War II and as an infantryman in the Israeli War of Independence, as well as in two other Israeli wars (1956 and 1973). Amichai was a university teacher, becoming a full-time writer after his retirement. He received the Israel Prize for Hebrew poetry in 1982, was poet in residence at Yale, Berkeley and NYU, and was honoured internationally. He published fiction and plays, many collections of poetry in Hebrew, and probably more collections in English translation than any other contemporary non-English poet.

Amichai gave readings in many countries, including the UK, notably at the first London Poetry International in 1967. Hughes collaborated with Amichai on three collections: *Selected Poems* (1968, with Assia Gutmann), *Amen* (1978) and *Time* (1979), the latter two translated with the Israeli poet himself.[1] In the last year of his life, Hughes and the present writer collaborated on a selection of English translations of Amichai's poetry (Faber, London, 2000).[2] Hughes was convinced that a generous selection of Amichai's poetry in English translation would guarantee him the Nobel Prize. These hopes, however, were not realized.

With time, it has become apparent that Amichai's was a distinctly modern enterprise, both in content and in language. As he himself put it, in his poem, "National Thoughts": "The language which described God and the Miracles, / Says: / Motor car, bomb, God." He draws also from the different historical stages of the language, ranging from Biblical Hebrew, through that of the Spanish Golden Age, to the contemporary and colloquial. The citation for the Israeli prize referred to "the revolutionary change in poetry's language" that he helped bring about, and indeed, though there is no Israeli laureateship, Amichai was closest to being the nation's chosen poet, in a practical sense as well, in that he was among the foremost creators of the modern

Hebrew language. In a 1992 interview he remarked: "I am, in a way, like the State of Israel – I have a poem which says, 'when I was young, the country was young'... My personal history has coincided with a larger history. For me it's always been one and the same." The American literary critic and scholar, Robert Alter, who has written extensively on this poet, points out that translatable as his work seems to be, much remains untranslatable.[3] As Alter notes, the apparent translatability of Amichai's poetry has even been held against the poet, perhaps with Robert Frost's dictum in mind: that it is the poetry itself that is lost in translation of poetry. It has even been claimed, as Alter puts it, that Amichai's "is the sort of meagre poetry in which nothing is lost in translation". On the other hand, it is arguable that Amichai belongs among the postwar poets of Europe who responded to devastations that seemed to have rendered traditional poetic devices less relevant. His language makes relatively few concessions to traditional means and devices, aspiring instead to a kind of universality, by definition more amenable perhaps to translation.

Ted Hughes learnt of Amichai's work in 1964, when the first issue of *Modern Poetry in Translation* was being prepared. I wrote to an English-language poet living in Jerusalem, Dennis Silk, asking him to identify and send samples of the work of leading contemporary Israeli poets. Silk submitted versions of several poems by Amichai, indicating that in his view Amichai was the best living Hebrew-language poet. These translations appeared in the first issue of *MPT* in 1965. In fact, the nine poems by Amichai that appeared there, including the longish poem, "King Saul and I", were the first items in that first issue of the journal. Heading the poems was a prose passage which Amichai himself, via Dennis Silk, had asked to be printed before his poems:

> *Joseph ben Matityahu (Josephus Flavius) was a field-commander of the Judaean Army in Galilee that fought Vespasian and Titus. He went over to the Romans and wrote the history of the campaign he had fought. He chose to write about what he had been involved in. I agree with Josephus. I want to be involved and avoid writing and then to be detached and write. The debate continues as to whether Josephus was, or was not, a traitor.*

So Amichai, it seems, believed that living came first and writing followed. Hana Amichai confirms (in an e-mail) that Yehuda repeated this dictum often and clearly felt strongly enough about it to want it included with his own poems, introducing his work in England. It appealed as well to Ted

Hughes who, much as he valued the writing life, also regarded it as secondary or auxiliary, in particular in his case, to environmental activism.

With his father, Hughes built a hut in his garden in Devon. He would retire there, in order, he once told me, "to rid the house of my idle presence". Idle he was not, and I recall him, in an earlier era, leaning against a mantelpiece writing, while Cambridge socialites surged about him. He had remarkable powers of concentration, which he sought to enhance by means of various disciplines. He was impressed, I recall, by a story about Schopenhauer, who wrote that the noise of carters cracking their whips in the street outside his house distracted him; Goethe too, apparently, before he would even set pen to paper, required total peace and assurance that he would not be disturbed. In perusing again the Hughes-Amichai correspondence, I came across the following by Hughes about one of Amichai's translators: "... an exceedingly likeable fellow but he's too stormy to translate. What a translator needs is pure calm – no distortion even of air-currents or water-currents." [4] Certainly, Hughes believed this of writing in general, even though he himself was capable of shutting out the distractions of the world.

Temperamentally, Hughes and Amichai were not dissimilar, although Amichai might not have been so rigorous about the necessary conditions for writing. Both were prolific writers, who apparently needed to write much, if they were to write at all; and both, in our parsimonious times, have inevitably been accused of over-productivity. Their appreciation of one another lent their relationship a fraternal quality, with Ted the junior and Yehuda the senior partner. Hughes's letters to Amichai suggest that he trusted the Israeli writer, sharing with him his enthusiasms and his fears; Amichai's letters to Hughes are somewhat more restrained, as befits the more worldly of the two. Hughes felt able to interpret Amichai's poetry and even asked him if he might translate his work: "Yehuda – if you have any hitch in getting a translator for your latest book would you mind letting me have a go at a few? You know I'd love to..." [5] But even before this, Hughes had been involved in the first substantial translation of Amichai's poetry into English, by Assia Gutmann. Gutmann also designed the cover of this book, using a transcription by herself of one of Amichai's poems in ancient Hebrew calligraphy. Hughes read her drafts and "combed them a little". At any rate, he later collaborated with Amichai himself and clearly relished this work.

One might speculate that Hughes's work on Amichai's poems – Amichai himself providing Hughes with literal versions – came at a critical point in his own life; the fact that Amichai was willing and able to provide versions in his own English was one reason for their collaboration being so extensive. Hughes made minimal changes, his object being to render the voice itself, audible in Amichai's self-translations, even more audible, or not to interfere with the existing audibility. He was engaged by the language, as deployed by someone whose knowledge of it was necessarily limited, and believed that its authenticity must be safeguarded. He himself had little difficulty "living with" the not-quite-standard English, and could resist the temptation to alter Amichai's text, so as to imprint the translation with his own style. There was indeed a selflessness in Hughes's approach, which seems to have had much to do with the friendship that developed between them. In his Introduction to *Amen*, he writes:

> *Amichai is the poet whose books I still open most often, take on a journey, most often return to when the whole business of writing anything natural, real and satisfying seems impossible. The effect his poetry has on me is to give me my own life – to open it up somehow, to make it all available to me afresh, to uncover all kinds of riches in every moment of it, and to free me from my mental prisons.*

The immediacy of Amichai's poetry accounts, too, for its popularity in his own country, where soldiers, it is reported, typically found room for a volume of his work in their kit-bags. But besides Amichai's naturalness, there was a sense of abundant inspiration, also greatly valued by Hughes. It is hardly surprising that he wanted to preserve above all "the tone and cadence of Amichai's own voice", there being no substitute. Since Amichai himself had pointed the way with English versions of his own work, Hughes needed to follow his lead. He went so far, once, as to chide the poet himself for attempting to render his translations more English-sounding.

The relationship between the two, however, as far as one can gather from the correspondence, confirms that Amichai was the senior partner. His sense of humour is apparent and, I think, was particularly appreciated by Hughes who certainly did not himself lack a sense of humour or of the absurd.

There are even more substantial reasons for the working and personal relationship between the two than an appreciation of each other's writing, essential though that must have been. As we have seen, Hughes was drawn to the writings of the first postwar generation of East European poets. Amichai was of that generation, his poetry also bearing the hallmark lucidity that characterized that of others of the same vintage. By involving himself, through translation, so closely with the Israeli poet's work, Hughes may be said to have apprenticed himself to this quality. That Amichai's work is so effective in English as well, has also to do with its focusing of historical experience, personalizing without trivializing.

Insistence on the sanctity of individual human life is characteristic of the work of many poets who survived a vicious war that took no account of individual victims, but Amichai, to an even greater extent than his coevals, talks to people from among people. That he was able to do so was maybe a function of his eminence as a national poet and one of the creators of a national language. Amichai's poetry resonates with Biblical imagery and associations, making the Bible contemporary, not by translating it literally but, paradoxically, by allowing the tradition to possess him, even as he also refuses to be overwhelmed by it. As Hughes himself commented to me, the Israeli poet deployed a poetic language of metaphor – a picture language – that operates clearly and powerfully behind the surface texture of words. The purity of this language survives translation, since the poet's evocation of images or pictures can be replicated between languages, even if the deeper associations of words resist the process.

It is indeed probably the pictorial quality of Amichai's work that has helped to make it so translatable, though his use of Biblical Hebrew to convey modern meanings is harder to convey. The un-translatability of his work has been commented on by various scholars of contemporary Hebrew literature, other than Robert Alter. Chana Kronfeld, for instance, whose co-translation with Chana Bloch of Amichai's last collection in English, *Open Closed Open*,[7] was much admired by Hughes, is intrigued by Amichai's translatability, "a puzzle since he writes so totally from within the textual echo chamber of Hebrew, and yet feels perfectly accessible in English". Amichai, like Hughes, regarded the ability to invent images as one of the triumphs of the human imagination, and it is not hard to see why poetry which evokes images should be more translatable. The means of so doing, it seemed to Hughes, was to avoid interposing oneself, eschewing the use of one's own stockpile of tricks and remedies. He felt even more strongly that a literalistic approach was indicated. Again one is reminded of T. S. Eliot's 1920 essay on Gilbert Murray's translations of classical Greek drama. If Murray represented one pole, Pound represented another, that of close attention to the rhythm and texture of sound, even at the expense of idiomatic usage. But most instructive for Hughes, perhaps, were the attempts by non-native speakers to render their own work in English. He paid particular attention to this, as we have seen, with Amichai – and later, via Csokits, with Pilinszky.

The other side of the partnership, that is, Amichai's intention to translate some of Ted Hughes's work into Hebrew, is less well known. (Amichai was greatly impressed by *Crow*, and did indeed translate some parts of it into Hebrew.) Certainly Amichai's letters to Hughes show a lively interest in and understanding of the latter's poetic accomplishments, albeit also drawing his attention to some dangers. In a letter to Hughes, for instance, he wrote:

> *As to your remarks about my poems, its strange that I feel towards your poems that they are real and concentrated like a landmine unexploded but filled with power [...] Whereas I feel about my things sometimes that they are like a mine after the explosion, scattered pieces. words. experiences, all strewn openly around for every one to see...*[8]

About *Gaudete* he wrote:

> *Gaudete (1977) arrived in a heat-wave in Jerusalem ... making me forget heat and political heat with a power I haven't experienced in a long time. I saw North Tawton* [the small town in which Hughes's Devon home was located] *and the way you said that under all this gentle greenery there are mounds and blood and wild prehistoric doings – So strange that after reading and reading it I had the feeling that I try to do the opposite in my things. Finding under all the burning ... a mystery of this country, some sweetness, gentleness ... We should change places for some time...*[9]

Much concerned with work that appeared to be therapeutically beneficial, one must suppose that Hughes felt translating Amichai's poems to be beneficial, intimating so on more than one occasion. In his introduction to *Amen*, at a time when he and I were preparing the first issue of *MPT* and were surveying the European poetry scene, comparing the Israeli poets with other poets of his generation located in Eastern Europe, he wrote:

> *In 1966, it was already noticeable that where the three poets from behind the Iron Curtain [Zbigniew Herbert, Miroslav Holub, Vasko Popa] gripped one's imagination and held one's awe, somehow Amichai's verse attracted and held one's affection as well. It became involved with one's intimate daily experience in a curious way.*

In a letter to Amichai himself, Hughes puts it even more forcefully.

> *Yehuda, I think you are my favourite poet – on one side there are all modern poets, writing the great intercontinental express of modern poetry, coaches crammed indiscriminately with great men, brilliant women, comedians, charlatans, ninnies, etc, but all racing along the flashing rails, a resounding 150 m.p.h. concatenation of modern*

poetry hurtling through the century, and on the other side there is you,
absolutely alone and apart from them – standing I imagine on a dusty
hill over Jerusalem – the sole shepherd of the voices of human beings.
You've discovered a subject that seems absolutely new to poetry, and it
turns out to be the human being speaking like a human being about
being a human being, or rather singing like one. The undiscovered
animal![10]

That Hughes did not, at this time, feel comfortable in England, where he was already a target for certain critics, is also evidenced by many letters in which he refers to the sense of being confined: "Here I am all twisted up in horrible England – it is a relief to think of you...." [11] He also indicated an eagerness to visit Israel: "I'm willing to go... to drag these tangled roots of mine out of their ugly bit of soil."

It is not hard, therefore, to see why, in particular with regard to Amichai, Hughes subscribed to a theory of minimal translation of poetry. Some at least of Hughes's motivation for beginning *MPT* stemmed from his conviction that what was needed was a boost for literal translation.

When it came to the translation of individual poems, however, this was more achievable than with plays, which had to function in the public arena as well. Hughes believed, as we have seen, that it was possible to render a poem in literal terms, although this might entail foregoing any attempt to repro-duce the form, regarded by some translators and many poets as a *sine qua non*. Instead, Hughes relied on his ability to select poems which already functioned in English, even in their literal form. If they seemed not to do so, he was less interested in becoming involved, perhaps because it meant that the temptation to compensate for the loss would become unavoidable. In fact, to describe Hughes's favoured tactic as "creative non-intervention" seems not far off the mark, self-control being essential, as well as the ability to understand or sense when a poem was "working", even in literalistic English translations, such as the versions occasionally provided by the source-language poet or by scholarly intimates.

Hughes's non-interventionist approach to translation matched what has sometimes been called the "minimalism" of the poetry of some of the poets of postwar Eastern and Central Europe. He repeatedly affirmed that he felt Amichai himself to be the best translator of his work. Of course, it is true that Amichai had an adequate command of English and was strongly influenced by English poetry. Hughes was quite explicit, both in his Introduction to *Amen* and in his letters to Amichai, about his role as a facilitator, rather than as a translator, on whose shoulders all responsibility rested. Very much to the point is his Introduction to *Amen*, in which reference is also made to Pound. To Amichai himself, he wrote, justifying his hands-off approach:

> *My problem is – that your translation has an idiom, and a tone, which is exactly you & which is very powerful poetry in itself, but which is just slightly strange in English ... The English of your translation is more like the English of somebody – some English body – with no literary education. Unspoiled, whole, life-size, natural etc. And with the oddity which is really you. So, I want to keep that. The whole warm, living impact of the poems depends on that. I saw 2 or 3 of your poems (of these poems in a magazine, where you had altered them more, anglicised them more, made them more "correct", but it seemed to me you'd knocked out some of the natural animal life – which the translations you sent me all have). So, I've simply corrected gross foreignisms. Otherwise, I've altered nothing. ...* [12]

Here, it is interesting that he had even taken the liberty, as noted earlier, of reprimanding Amichai himself for surrendering to the demand for "normalization" of his English texts. One might suppose that Amichai, a teacher after all, might have bridled at the comment that his English was "more like the English of somebody... with no literary education". At the same time, one can see what Hughes had in mind. In the editorial to *MPT* 3, Spring 1967, he laid down what he hoped would be an enduring tendency of the magazine, expressing his belief in self-translation, however inadequate the poet's knowledge of English. One appreciates, too, what Hughes meant by a translation crib, the loving care called for when translating a foreign original:

> *[W]e feel more strongly than ever that the first ideal is 'literalness', insofar as the original is what we are curious about. The very oddity and struggling dumbness of a word-for-word version is what makes our own imagination jump. A man who has something really serious to say in a language of which he knows only a few words, manages to say it far more convincingly and effectively than any interpreter and in translated poetry, it is the first hand contact – however fumbled and broken – with that man and his seriousness which we want. The minute we gloss his words, we have more or less what he said but we have lost him. We are ringing changes – amusing though they may be – on our own familiar abstractions, and are no longer reaching through to what we have not experienced before, which is alive and real.*

That he had Amichai in mind seems certain. The latter, again, might not have relished epithets like "fumbled and broken" or "struggling dumbness" but it was his awareness or perception of the value of these qualities that made Hughes opt for non-intervention, creative in my view, because only someone as convinced as he was would have perceived the need to leave intact what Amichai had expressed, making only minimal changes that a copy-editor might feel compelled to make. On the other hand, some intervention may seem desirable, the problem being not how much, but when there was enough. Although his own versions are not self-indulgent, in the ordinary sense of the term, it is apparent that working with Amichai's accomplished but still not contemporarily idiomatic English interested Hughes at a time when he was searching for an English less weighed down by historic-cultural and class accretions. In the search for a more direct means of communication, Hughes sought to renew or refine, to simplify what was his own inherited manner, owing something to the elaborations, for instance, of the American poet John Crowe Ransom as well as, more obviously, to the grittiness of Gerard Manley Hopkins.

In returning to the methodology adopted in working with Amichai, it must be remembered that this followed Hughes's more tentative role as reader of and co-worker in Assia Gutmann's translations. These also drew on Amichai's drafts, although Gutmann had enough Hebrew to read the poems in the source language as well and so was less dependent on Amichai's own renderings than was Hughes later. A couple of examples will suffice. In the poem, "Letter of Recommendation", Hughes made only two minor changes to Amichai's draft.[13] In stanza 3, altering the preposition in "to my father" to "from my father"; and in the last stanza changing "may he be woken up" to "let him be woken up". So, he clearly does what he claims to be doing, correcting errors of usage, albeit very slight. On the other hand, Hughes has left some of Amichai's characteristically not quite colloquial locutions, for instance, in stanza 1: "On summer nights I sleep naked / in Jerusalem on my bed / which stands on the brink / of a deep valley / without rolling down into it." This is not incorrect, but though it might be somewhat more colloquial to say: "which stands on the brink of a deep valley and does not roll down into it", Hughes was determined to keep it as Amichai had it, except in cases of unquestionable error or unintentional ambiguity. As for "Letter of Recommendation", Amichai's version is written out again by Hughes without any change, apart from the second of the two changes mentioned above: one supposes to make it more readable but also, perhaps, to absorb it more completely, since Hughes firmly believed in a connection between the pen-holding hand and the mind (the reason he gave for not using a word-processor). I suspect that he was uncertain about the preposition since "a letter ... of my father" has certain resonances that the more explicit "letter ... from my father" lacks. The handwritten copy of Amichai's version is accompanied by a typed copy, with the second change introduced, but not the first, although the printed version contains both changes. It is true that some of the other versions are more altered than this, but still not radically changed from Amichai's drafts.

Evidently, then, Hughes saw his role as relatively unintrusive. This accords little with our notion of the poet at work, and it may be hard to accept. It required considerable boldness or self-discipline not to intervene, when intervention might have been the easier as well as being the approved course. However, it may well have been assumed by critics and others, receiving these versions from so renowned a poet as Ted Hughes, that he had intervened substantially. When publishers were made aware that Hughes was not working alone, his translations were sometimes criticized as being straitjacketed. But no one knew what was really happening with regard to these translations, the circumstances of which were ideal, in that Amichai's knowledge of English was so good and there was a bond of sympathy between the poets.

Nevertheless, it will be instructive to look at one of Hughes's translations, where the opposite takes place. The poem "A Dog After Love", a typically irreverent Amichai poem and a good example of Hughes's tendency not to interfere with the poet's own draft.[14] The Ted Hughes archive at Emory University includes a copy in Amichai's hand, a fair copy in Hughes's hand, and a typed copy. There is no revision at all in this case. Amichai's draft is as follows: "After you left me / I let a dog smell at / My chest and my belly. It will fill its nose / And set out to find you. // I hope it will tear the / Testicles of your lover and bite off his penis / Or at least / Will bring me your stockings between his teeth." This has been transcribed by Hughes, followed by a typescript of the same, presumably also by Hughes. What is apparent is Hughes's determination to preserve *everything* in the Amichai version, including the problematical lineation. For good measure, here is another poem, "Of Three or Four in a Room". The Burnshaw literal version, from his anthology *The Poem Itself,*[15] is below, with the translation by Gutmann and Hughes in italics.[16]

Out of Three or Four in the Room

Of three or four in the room
Out of three or four in a room
One is always standing at the window,
One is always standing by the window
[He] must see injustice among the thorns
Forced to see the injustice amongst the thorns,
And the fires [burning] on the hills.
The fires on the hill.

And how men who departed whole
And people who left whole
Are brought back to their home in the evening like small change.
Are brought home in the evening, like small change.

Of three or four in a room
Out of three or four in a room
[There is] always one [who is] standing by the window.
One is always standing at the window.
His dark hair above [upon] his thoughts.
Hair dark above his thoughts,
Behind him, words.
Behind him, the words.
And before him voices that wander without a knapsack,
And in front of him the words, wandering, without luggage,
Hearts without provisions, prophecies without water,
Hearts without provision, prophecies without water
And large stones that have been returned
And big stones put there
And remain unopened like letters that have no
And staying, closed, like letters
Address and no recipient.
With no addresses; and no one to receive them.

Amichai, unlike Hughes, had personal experience of war, even if, arguably, Hughes was a kind of leftover First World War poet, having vicariously experienced the rigours of combat through his father's accounts . At any rate, Hughes's vision did not eschew these aspects of twentieth-century historical experience. As A. Alvarez said of *Crow* in an *Observer* review, : "With *Crow*, Hughes joins the select band of survivor-poets whose work is adequate to the destructive reality we inhabit." By "select band", Alvarez was referring to poets of Eastern Europe, especially perhaps Zbigniew Herbert of Poland, whose work Alvarez himself had endorsed and introduced, as a separate volume in the "Penguin Modern European Poets" series, of which he was Advisory Editor.

Amichai was of that generation and, to some extent, of that company, but his experience was somewhat different. Hughes wrote of this, in his Introduction to *Amen*, referring to the first issue of *MPT* and specifically to Herbert, Holub, and Popa; his identification with Amichai is apparent. Inevitably, the English poet was criticized for simplifying the political situation in Eastern Europe. But he was not, after all, addressing specialists, he was trying to engage the attention of a larger audience. His introduction, in fact, manages to convey some aspects of Amichai's creative life and the forces that shaped it, as well as to express his personal esteem for this work.

Distinct forms of English exist in places other than the mother country, where the breakdown of the class-system means that there is no longer a universally recognized, correct or standard form of the language. For this reason, since examples of diverse usage abound, British English is more hospitable than other languages to foreign importations. Nevertheless, did Hughes really expect it to be believed that all he had to do was "correct the more intrusive oddities and errors of grammar and usage...."? I suspect that he was aware, even in those comparatively innocent times, that this stated limitation on his intervention was likely to be seen as controversial and maybe even misleading. Since then, and since Hughes's death, the tide has turned somewhat, at least academically, but has if anything turned in the opposite direction. "Foreignization" may have validated the literalist or non-interventionist approach to translation, but the cult of the creative personality has made it almost inconceivable that a poet of Hughes's stature would engage in an enterprise in which his function appeared to be so limited. My own investigations confirm that his description of what he saw as his function was accurate.

I was struck recently by a remark by Neil Roberts, in his study of Ted Hughes:

To have adapted or taken liberties with the work of poets who had this
kind of importance to Hughes would have violated the spirit of his
interest in them, and he settled for literalness as a first principle.
Where Hughes is working from a literal translation of a poem in a
language he does not know, this principle seems paradoxical – what
can Hughes contribute? [17]

This bemusement is understandable, but what Hughes perhaps contributed is more conveniently defined in negative terms: a determination *not* to interfere with what he felt was an authentic and compelling voice, *not* to impose his own reading or substitute his own voice, even if it could be claimed he was speaking in accents he would not have adopted had he not encountered the particular source text. It takes particular acuteness of perception to hear authenticity, as does Hughes in the case of Amichai's English rendering of his own work, including the Israeli poet's particular intonation, his blend of irony, humility and pride.

A greater willingness today to accept foreign-sounding versions would perhaps have been more favourable to Hughes's non-interventionist tactics. Poets seems to have taken over the translation of poetry, the assumption being that only a poet can translate poetry and that what is required, given the manifest problems in doing so, is a kind of re-creation. Hughes, determined to resist such temptations, placed his talents at the disposal of the poets whose works he admired, by providing subtly worked literalistic versions. Since for Hughes, literal versions often did the job best, he typically made minimal modifications or "Englishing", which preserved their effect. The minimal "Englishing" that he did undertake required sensitivity to the language, which should not be underestimated. But behind this was a belief in the permeability of language, the ability of poets of this postwar generation to transcend linguistic boundaries; it was this belief on which *Modern Poetry in Translation* was based.

.

III
János Pilinszky
The Troubled Mechanic

Budapest-born, János Pilinszky (1921-1981) published plays, scripts and prose, besides poetry. During the Second World War, he spent several months in prisoner-of-war camps. His first collection of poems, *Trapéz és Korlát / Trapeze and Parallel Bars* (1946), won him the prestigious Baumgarten Prize. Other volumes followed, and in 1971 he was awarded the Attila József Prize for *Nagyvárosi Ikonok / Metropolitan Icons* (1970). From 1946 to 1948 he had co-edited *Újhold*, a modernist literary and critical journal. However, with the Communist takeover of Hungary, this journal was banned and Pilinszky was silenced for over a decade. His 1964 oratorio *Sötét mennyország / Dark Heaven* was set to music by Endre Szervánszky. Pilinszky also wrote several avant-garde filmscripts reminiscent of Beckett's work. In 1977 he published his thoughts about his relationship with Sheryl Sutton, the black artist and member of Robert Wilson's Paris-based company. [1]

In a commemorative essay, "János Pilinszky: A Very Different Poet", Pilinszky's contemporary, the poet Ágnes Nemes Nagy, described the poems appearing in the poet's first volume as already among the "future basic poems of the new Hungarian literature."[2] She wrote:

> *The war has ended and the gates of the concentration camps are shut, but I believe that it is precisely this final hush which signifies the supreme reality in our midst today... Pilinszky is different. Everybody is different but some are even more so. Pilinszky is deviant, rare and improbable, a white antelope, an element beyond the periodic table. When he walked down the street, one of those dark Budapest streets of the Fifties, in his short coat, too tight at the shoulders, he was like a persecuted legend. And that is just what he was! A persecuted legend, expelled from literature and totally unknown; fellow-dwellers in the catacombs maybe whispered his name, passing it from mouth to mouth and ear to ear.*

Ted Hughes, who first met Pilinszky at the second Poetry International in

London in 1969, echoes and expands on this assessment when he writes of Pilinszky's poetry:

> The silence of artistic integrity 'after Auschwitz' is a real thing. The mass of the human evidence of the camps, and of similar situations since, has screwed up the price of 'truth' and 'reality' and 'understanding' beyond what common words seem able to pay. [...] The poems are nothing if not part of an appeal to God, but it is a God who seems not to exist. [...] A god of absences and negative attributes, quite comfortless. A god in whose creation the camps and modern physics are equally at home. But this God has the one Almightiness that matters: he is the Truth.[3]

Hughes, too, saw Pilinszky as different from other postwar generation poets from Central Europe. He tried to characterize the Hungarian poet's work, in a tribute to his co-translator, writing that what attracted him to Pilinszky's poems was "their air of simple, helpless accuracy". This does not, of course, mean that he felt the poems were simple, but that to Pilinszky had been revealed the truth of our final condition, "a truth often ignored". Hughes notes that "the intensity is not forced or strenuous, in any way; it is, rather, a stillness and at the same time an ecstasy of affliction, a glare of inner exposure, a passivity of transfiguration."[3]

His own language reflects his spiritual closeness to Pilinszky, always remembering that he read the latter's work through the prism of János Csokits's scrupulous versions. What Hughes intimated, Pilinszky had experienced. It is the effulgent quality in Pilinszky's work, "the glare of inner exposure" that focuses Hughes's attention, so that his own versions of Pilinszky's poems display an almost dazzled intensity of perception that marked also his own poetry. Hughes outlines the genesis of his and Csokits's translation of Pilinszky's poetry, stressing his co-translator's dedication to the work and missionary determination to break through the sound-barrier around the Hungarian language – Hungarian being, of course, a kind of linguistic orphan in Central and Eastern Europe, which is dominated by Slavic languages and German, the *lingua franca* of the region. The Hungarian PEN Club fostered translation of Hungarian works of literature, offering bursaries and attracting distinguished English-language writers (e.g., Edwin Morgan) who were encouraged, with the help of Hungarian writers, to translate Hungarian works. Csokits, an émigré, without official backing or incentives, was nevertheless similarly dedicated to this task, especially to the work of his contemporary János Pilinszky.

János Csokits was also a friend of Ted Hughes who had persuaded Csokits to guest-edit a Hungarian issue of *MPT* and to collaborate with him on the translation, for this issue initially, of some Hungarian poets of the first post-war generation, Pilinszky prominent among them. Hughes, meanwhile, had been much impressed by another Hungarian poet, Ferenc Juhász, especially by one of his poems, "The Boy Changed into a Stag Cries Out at the Gate of Secrets", though this poet was not one Csokits greatly admired. [4] Ágnes Nemes Nagy, among the poets selected by Csokits for the putative Hungarian issue of *MPT*, has been quoted above. Lajos Koncz, too, cites a letter received from Hughes, accompanying some translations.[5] Hughes's letter draws particular attention to Csokits's role in the translation of Pilinszky's poetry:

[A]s you will see, they are pretty literal. In fact my co-translator, János Csokits, has let me get away with very little. He insisted on the closest verbal accuracy. This was very much to my own taste. We have tin-kered with most of them for nearly eight years. Quite a few of them now satisfy me completely as English poems. I am extremely pleased with them. Others are at least accurate and effective, though I feel I could go on altering and adjusting my versions of them forever...

The mixture of tentativeness, satisfaction, confidence and pride even in the results, is striking. As Hughes significantly says, in his introduction to the volume of Pilinszky's selected poems: "Nothing conveys that [he had alluded to "the air of simple, helpless accuracy"] so well as the most literal crib. And I suppose if we had the audacity that is what we should be printing here. As it is, we settle for literalness as a first principal." Pilinszky's verse would have been betrayed, Hughes was convinced, by anything less than verbal accuracy. He kept making slight adjustments, but also notes that he was constantly nudged back to what Csokits had produced in the first place.

Although Ted Hughes does not write systematically about the translation process, he did compose a piece on his collaboration with Csokits. His remarks on this collaboration are worth quoting fully as they seem to oppose the more commonly accepted strategy of aligning the translated poetry with the translator's original writing. Hughes vividly describes the awakening of his interest in Pilinszky's poetry, as virtually dictating his approach:

I am certain I would never have become as interested in Pilinszky as I eventually did, if my curiosity had not been caught in the first place by Csokits' swift word-for-word translations from the page at odd times during our long friendship. ... But even more exciting, for me, was the knack he had of projecting a raw, fresh sense of the strange original –

the particular and to me alien uniqueness of the original. ... Faithful-
ness to the original is crucial in translating Pilinszky's poetry. [6]

Self-limitation constitutes an alternative procedure, requiring strict control
if not suppression of the urge to colonize the source text, even if Ezra Pound
seemed to recommend that process as one of "making it new", bringing it to
life for the reader by first bringing it to life for oneself, by making it one's own.
Robert Lowell's statement on this account became something of a bench-
mark for later discussions of poetry translation.[7] Alluding frankly to his
intentions, taking as a precedent the tradition of "imitation", as evinced and
described by Dryden, Lowell illustrates his contentions, citing the Russian
poet Boris Pasternak, whose novel *Dr Zhivago* had become a *cause célèbre*.
Pasternak was celebrated in Russia primarily on account of his poetry,
but also for his translations, which included some of Shakespeare's plays
(*Hamlet, Macbeth, King Lear*), Goethe's *Faust*, and work by Rilke, Verlaine
and some Georgian poets. His translations of Shakespeare were popular with
the Russian public partly on account of their modernized dialogues,
although critics also accused him of "pasternakizing" Shakespeare. Awarded
the Nobel Prize for Literature in 1958, Pasternak at first accepted the award,
but soon, under political pressure, sent the Swedish Academy a telegram
rejecting it. The Swedish Academy, for its part, announced that this refusal in
no way altered the validity of the award, Pasternak having declined to accept
it under threat of expulsion from his native land. Lowell's allusion to the
embattled author thus constituted an expression of support as well as indicating a concurrence with the Russian author's views on translation.
However, it should be pointed out that Pasternak's approach was not
unorthodox in the context of Russian literature in the English-speaking
world, though at the time it offered a challenge to academic literalism. Early
in Lowell's Preface to his *Imitations* comes the following:

Boris Pasternak has said that the usual reliable translator gets the lit-
eral meaning but misses the tone, and that in poetry, tone is of course
everything. I have been reckless with literal meaning, and laboured
hard to get the tone. Most often this has been a tone, for the tone is some-
thing that will always more or less escape transference to another lan-
guage and cultural moment. I have tried to write alive English and to
do what my authors might have done if they were writing their poems
now and in America.

... Strict metrical translators still exist. ... Their difficulties are bold
and honest, but they are taxidermists, not poets, and their poems are

likely to be stuffed birds. A better strategy would seem to be the now
fashionable translations into free or irregular verse. ... I believe that
poetic translation – I would call it an imitation – must be expert and
inspired, and needs at least as much technique, luck and rightness of
hand as an original poem.[7]

Though Ted Hughes's approach was certainly not academic, he was doubtful about Lowell's subjectivism. Hughes aspired to preserve the uniqueness or foreignness of the source texts, and his Introduction to the Pilinszky selection expresses this just as forcefully as Lowell had expressed his point of view in his Preface to *Imitations*. Here is what Hughes has to say about the literal texts:

Very many lines of his [Csokits's] rough draft have been impossible to
improve, as far as I could judge, and besides that odd inevitability and
'style' which a poet's translation into a language other than his own
often seems to have ..., [Csokits] retained naturally an unspoiled sense
of the flavour and the tone of the originals — that very intriguing qual-
ity which is the translator's will-o'-the-wisp, the foreignness and
strangeness. That most important thing was something I developed a
feeling for, wherever János Csokits captured it, but I could not begin to
re-invent it where he did not, or where I had to re-align his wording.
Instead, I was too often conscious of reducing Pilinszky to the worn
tracks and familiar locutions of workaday English. The best way to
escape this claustrophobic feeling of locking up foreign uniqueness in
home-grown commonplace, is to re-invent—so that the over-drive
exhilaration of new imagination freshens the task. This way I decided
not to take.[8]

It seems, then, that Hughes was indeed tempted by Lowell's rationale for his "imitations", but resisted it. Clearly, he did not see his role as that of re-invention but rather of preservation, building on or adjusting what Csokits had already achieved, an achievement to which he paid tribute. What Ted Hughes was contributing was in fact something often almost invisible to critics and still not fully appreciated. It relates to a sense of indebtedness to poets of Pilinszky's generation as well as to Hughes's conviction that he could learn only by following in their footsteps.

His endeavour, then, was to register, rather than revise or rewrite, even if translation inevitably involves at least some rewriting . Hughes had got to know Pilinszky's poetry through ad-verbum versions which convinced him that here was a poet whose work, if not, as he put it, reduced "to the worn tracks and familiar locution of workaday English", might transcend or survive translation. He felt that translation of Pilinszky's poetry was best accomplished therefore by allowing his co-translators' draft versions or cribs to govern the proceedings. He did not follow the route of "re-invention", a route which was commonly urged on him, not least by the advisors to his publishers. The route he did follow was described by him in what amounts to a translational credo:

> *[T]he very thing that attracted me to Pilinszky's poems in the first place was their air of simple helpless accuracy. Nothing conveys that so well as the most literal crib, and I suppose if we had the audacity that is what we should be printing here. As it is, we settled for* literalness *as a* first principle.[9]

Hughes's essay in *Translating Poetry: The Double Labyrinth* is as good a statement as any of his intentions in translating poetry. He also doubtless regarded himself as fortunate, having in the first instance Amichai's own renderings of his work and in the second renderings by a close friend and admirer of Pilinszky, as well as access to both poets. It is not known to what extent Hughes and Pilinszky conferred, but in any case, Csokits would surely have conveyed to his fellow-countryman and poet any queries Hughes may have had and, as noted, Hughes and Pilinszky were able to communicate directly in French.

János Csokits alerted me to the existence of a 1976 BBC recording of a "round-table discussion" between Hughes, Pilinszky, Csokits, and László Jotischky, then head of the Hungarian Section of the BBC World Service at Bush House.[10] The three Hungarian participants spoke in Hungarian and their comments were translated into English by Jotischky for Hughes's benefit. Some excerpts are quoted below, as is Csokits's ad-verbum version of the first two stanzas of a poem written by Pilinszky in 1947, "The French Prisoner", together with the accompanying notes, prepared by Csokits for Hughes's information. Hughes's final version of the poem, based on materials he received, appears in the collection of Pilinszky's poems titled *The Desert of Love*.[11]

> JOTISCHKY: ... *Ted, what led you to this undertaking? Why did you choose a Hungarian poet, and why exactly János Pilinszky?*
> HUGHES: *I came to János Pilinszky's poems through János Csokits, whom I suppose I first met in 1960. He must have translated very roughly one or two of János Pilinszky's poems in '61, '62, or '63, because*

these poems were his great passion. And I was immediately taken with them, and saw in these very rough translations a most unusual and fine kind of English poem which interested me greatly. I was curious to see how final a poem in English I could make it. And so over the next few years we translated more and more. But it was through János Csokits that I originally found them.

JOTISCHKY: *You said you saw a fine English poem in them. I often wonder how a poet who does not speak a language can translate poetry from that language. How can you feel the music, the emotional contents, the atmosphere of the poem?*

HUGHES: *It's a mystery. But I think there are several kinds of music in a poem. There is a verbal music, right at the surface; there is a rhythm, a meter, the actual structure of the verse; there is also a rhythm of phrases, a music of cadences, of intonations, of emotions. And I suppose, finally, too, there's a music of the progression of ideas. I think the first of these, the music of the language, is something that you cannot hope to translate. The moment you begin to try to translate that, you get curiosities, maybe very interesting curiosities, like some of Ezra Pound's translations, but you do not get the poem. The other, the music of intonations, the music of the emotions, is something which reappears in every language just as the emotion itself does. And the music of the progression of the ideas is always evident, like mathematics – that you can translate. If there is a very strong element of that kind of music in a poem, it is usually quite translatable.*

JOTISCHKY: *János, ...when you take this book, with its attractive blue and yellow cover into your hands, how can you be sure that it is really you in English, that it does not distort your poetry?*

PILINSZKY: *... This is rather embarrassing for me! Obviously there has been a meeting of the minds, via poetry. First with János Csokits and then with Ted Hughes. János became a link between us, because, I think, of the thoroughness and accuracy of his translation of my poems, in which Ted Hughes, amazingly, found himself at home. I had already realized that in 1967, when we first met, and then even more in 1969, when we discussed some translations – these were not yet based on János Csokits' roughs and there were parts in the text which might easily have been misunderstood. Well, Ted Hughes questioned me with the confidence of a guide in a labyrinth, who already knows the way. ...*

JOTISCHKY: *...So what you are saying is that it is not so much language* *that separates one poet from the other, but the fact that they are two different persons. ... And as a good teacher, you could tell from his questions that he understood.*

PILINSZKY: *I had known several of Ted Hughes' poems, also from rough translations. I have always wanted to translate his poems and still do, but have felt it was beyond my capacity. It is very interesting what separates and what links us. His way of thinking is a bit more mythological, while mine is rather metaphysical.*

...

HUGHES: *In English, translations have certainly played an enormous part, sometimes the most significant part. The most important work in English literature, and the biggest influence, must be the Bible, which is a translated poem really. And each period of revival in English literature usually coincided with a great deal of translation; this obviously somehow fed the literary activity of the particular time. Some of the most interesting poetry now in English is translated. Clearly it is a legitimate form.*

JOTISCHKY: *What about in Hungarian? To what extent is the translation a new piece of work and comparable to the original? ...*

PILINSZKY: *This is a difficult question. A translation becomes an original work by virtue of being the same as the original. How shall I put it? ... I think the big challenge in translation is to feel the personality of the other. Consider the poem as a game of chess. This game is played within a given culture, and it is the game of a given personality. Now we have to intervene in this game. It has to be transferred into another language. ...*

There are original poems, for instance, which – and this is usually meant pejoratively – feel like translations, even though they are original works. And there are translations which are perfectly self-sufficient, but not because they are not accurate, not necessarily because of that.

JOTISCHKY: *If a poem of yours is translated into different languages, the end results may be different. You have already been translated into various languages. Can you compare the translations? Do you feel that your poems have been translated differently?*

PILINSZKY: *It's very hard to say. Because even if I read a translation of my own poem in a foreign language I understand, I know my own poem so well that it shows through the translation to the point where I cannot separate the two. And in the foreign language, obviously, one cannot find one's way about so well...*

...

JOTISCHKY: *...I'd like to ask Ted Hughes the mirror image of that question. Ted, I was just asking János how far he takes into consideration the language into which the poem is being translated; I mean by this not only the English language, as in this case, but also the poet-translator's poetic language. I would like to ask you how far the language of the original influences you, when you are putting a translation into its final English form? Does the fact of your knowing or not knowing the original language, the tone of the language, influence you?*

HUGHES: *I think not at all. With these poems, for instance, I had a very strong sense of the tone. But whether my sense of the tone was that of the original language is something that I cannot tell; I do not know Hungarian. Nevertheless, János Csokits's rough English renderings, very literal English renderings, extremely evocative and often very precise and good English, were very difficult to improve on in any way. From them I got a very clear and strong feeling of a definite tone, temper in the language, a definite temper in the way of speaking, the voice. I could work with this, as with something very solid. But I think it was far removed from the actual verbal surface of the original poems.*

JOTISCHKY: *In other words, what you ended with was a collection of English poems, written by a Hungarian.*

HUGHES: *It is a collection of English poems in that I think many of these are poems, maybe all of them, a good few, I think, are among the best poems I have written and maybe better than most that I have written. So, in that sense, they are finished English poems. But they are also absolutely literal. Mr Csokits made quite sure that I should not wander in the slightest. I took no liberties at all, and to draw that kind of literal word-for-word rendering into something that has all the finish of an original poem in our language was just a matter of time.*

JOTISCHKY: *And when you look at any one of these poems, do you feel that it is your own as much as János's or János's?*

HUGHES: *It does not seem strange to me, it seems very familiar. And yet it is something I would never have got to myself, something I have extended myself towards, rather than produced out of myself. I have not turned János Pilinszky's poems into my poems; I have adapted myself in some way to something that attracted me strongly.*

JOTISCHKY: *Can it be said that these poems are the result, the happy result I hasten to add, of a sort of collaboration of three poets?*

HUGHES: *I think so. As I was saying, much of János Csokits's version was unalterable. It was so immediate in its final poetic effect that I didn't change it. There are many lines of that sort in the book. But at the same time, János Csokits was somehow locating something in János Pilinszky very, very accurately, which I could feel as quite distinct, quite unlike any other poet. Quite unlike János Csokits. And so the three of us managed to establish a very close link, often getting very close, with a minimum of shifts and arrangements. But what, of course, we lost completely in English was the surface music and the actual Hungarian tension of the surface of the poem, that being a great deal of any poem. So what we have translated is the skeleton, the internal works of the poem. Nevertheless, in English the poems acquired a surface of a completely different kind from János Pilinszky's, but a surface nevertheless – I suppose that surface is mine.*

JOTISCHKY: *... This brings me to my last question, primarily directed at János Pilinszky. Do you think it is possible to create translations of this calibre if the translator does not like the original poem or its author?*

PILINSZKY: *Well, I haven't thought a lot about that. ... But it is not impossible. It is not impossible, because, even if the result is not likely to be so good, an opportunity is created for virtuosity. This can happen with actors who may be best in roles that are not so good. It gives some kind of freedom, lightness. If the translator is a good poet, as I've just said, an opportunity for virtuosity is created. ... But I would not think that it is possible without some love or inner desire.*

...

JOTISCHKY: *... Now, Ted, just to put you in the picture. I asked the two Hungarian poets whether they thought it was possible to produce a valid literary translation of a poem which they didn't like, or a poem written by a poet they didn't like, as a poet, or as a person. The answer seems to be that while it may be possible as a virtuoso act, a sort of trial of strength, it is not the real thing, it will never produce a real poem. What do you feel about this?*

HUGHES: *I'd agree with that. I think it would be impossible to give enough of yourself to make a new poem in your own language. I think it would just be a curiosity, an exercise.*

JOTISCHKY: *Have you ever tried to translate something that you did not really like?*

HUGHES: *Yes. I have translated a good deal of what I did not particularly like, that I was merely curious to turn into English from French. But it remained a curiosity, and I was never able, I was never interested enough, to try and take it further. Had I concentrated on any single piece, I imagine it would have fallen apart. I could not have made it cohere. It's hard to know how you could do this except as a toy, as if you were constructing a toy. ...*

Finally, "The French Prisoner", Csokits's draft version and notes followed by Hughes's version:

Csokits ad-verbum:

If only I could forget him, that Frenchman, who,
towards dawn, I saw creeping in front
of our quarters in the thicket of the backyard,
so that he almost grew into the ground.
Peering around he glanced back just then,
and having at last found a safe hide-out:
now [1] his grab [2] can be [1] his completely!
Whatever happens, he won't move farther on.

Already he was eating it, devouring the turnip [3],
which he must have smuggled out [4] under his rags.
He was eating raw cattle-turnip [3], but he had hardly
swallowed one mouthful, before it came up again;
and the sweet food met on his tongue
with disgust and pleasure in the same way
as the happy and the unhappy meet
in their insatiable [5] carnal ecstasy [5]!

Notes:

Again I tried not to be "literary" but rather literal. However, there is a limit beyond which, I feel, a word-for-word translation would need so many explanatory notes that I had to exclude it, not without regret. But my main concern was not to "write poetry" ... but to give you well-

prepared material for the real translation job. I tried to be as close as possible. ...

1 and 2. In the first stanza Pilinszky suddenly changes from past to present tense – mainly to make you feel as the fugitive did – does – and I think in Hungarian the thing works marvellously well. I added the word "now" for clarity. [The Hungarian word] means: spoil, plunder etc... I chose "grab" in view of the turnip!

3. In the typewritten text you gave I found "mangel-wurzel" but I prefer "turnip" and "cattle-turnip" which are closer to the Hungarian original and sound less "Academy of Agriculture".

4. In Hungarian the word is "stole", abbreviation for "stole out" but "smuggle out" is the clear meaning.

5. "insatiable" is the nearest adjective I could find and I hope that "insatiable ecstasy" is a possible expression in English. "Ecstasy" feels nearer to the original than "rapture" – particularly because of the full text – "insatiable carnal ecstasy"...

Hughes's final version:

If only I could forget that Frenchman.
I saw him a little before dawn, creeping past our hut
into the dense growth of the back garden
so that he almost merged into the ground.
As I watched he looked back, he peered all round –
at last he had found a safe hideout.
Now his plunder can be all his!
Whatever happens, he'll go no further.

And already he is eating, biting into the turnip
which he must have smuggled out under his rags.
He was gulping raw cattle-turnip!
Yet he had hardly swallowed one mouthful
before it vomited back up.
Then the sweet pulp in his mouth mingled
with joy and revulsion the same
as the happy and unhappy are coupled
in their bodies' ravenous ecstasy.

In the first place, Hughes's caution is evident; he is concerned lest he inadvertently offend his interlocutors, and he is also anxious to give credit where it is due, primarily to János Csokits, the mediator between the source texts and his own attempts to recreate the poem in English, without converting it into a poem of his own. But even more significant is Hughes's indication of what he feels may be brought across, this not being the "music of the words", for many the distinguishing feature of poetry, but the "progression of ideas". Hughes, in fact, loses no time in trying to reproduce what, by definition, he felt could not be reproduced, that is, the "verbal music" of the source text; however, he points out that the "music of intonation, of the emotion, is something which reappears in every language just as the emotion itself does." This is surely verifiable as regards a European poet whose historical ordeal may well be imagined by an English poet old enough to remember World War II. The music of the "progression of ideas", as Hughes claims, is always evident, "like mathematics", and this, he believed, was translatable; it was this "music" that he also found in the poetry of some of his slightly older, Central European contemporaries. Csokits refers to Hughes ability to 'x-ray' poems, and Hughes himself talks of translating "the skeleton, the internal works of a poem".

At this point, it will help to look at one of the annotated texts Csokits prepared for Hughes's use and at the "final" version as published in the Carcanet and Anvil editions of the selected poems. Hughes preserved all Csokits's notes and commentaries and their correspondence dealing with the translation of Pilinszky's poetry, so that there is an unusually comprehensive archive of this project. Apparent is how openly Hughes describes the process and indeed how crucial are the Csokits literals, an example of which Hughes would have liked to include in his Introduction. Hughes is describing a process markedly different to that which typically occurs, where the final version seeks, rather, to distance itself from the literal or initial one. Here is Csokits's "crib" of and notes to another poem, "On the Wall of a KZ-Lager", the Hungarian source text of which was available to Hughes, who also heard it recited by Csokits and by Pilinszky himself. This short poem purports to record the terminal sentiments of a victim, from within the prison itself:

Where you have fallen here you remain.
From the universe you have this place
Just this single place,
But this one you have really acquired

The country side is fleeing you
Whether a house, a mill or a poplar,
All things just grapple with you,
As if they were mutating in nothingness.

But now it is you who won't give way
Did we blind you? You keep us in sight.
Did we rob you? You enriched yourself,
Speechless, speechless you accuse us.

Hughes's final version is as follows:

Where you have fallen, you stay.
In the whole universe, this is your place.
Just this single spot.
But you have made this yours absolutely.

The countryside evades you.
House, mill, poplar,
Each thing strives to be free of you
as if it were mutating in nothingness.

But now it is you who stay.
Did we blind you? You continue to watch us.
Did we rob you? You enriched yourself.
Speechless, speechless, you testify against us.

IV
European Poets, Past and Present

Ted Hughes's interest in translation, encouraged by the reception of *Modern Poetry in Translation*, already envisaged several ambitious projects. Helder Macedo, a prominent Portuguese poet and a Fellow of King's College London, with his wife Suzette, collaborated with Hughes on the translation of a poem by Fernando Pessoa's friend and colleague Mário de Sá Carneiro for a Portuguese issue of *MPT*. Hughes also translated poems by Macedo himself for this issue. As was his custom, he his collaborators to provide as literal or non-literary translations as they could bring themselves to undertake, though he took care not to offend anyone by seeming to ride roughshod over literary sensibilities. Letters from Ted Hughes to Suzette and Helder Macedo stress his non-interventionist approach, but he still wondered if he was not taking too many liberties. Thus, he wrote to Suzette, asking as usual for "word-by-word transcriptions":

> *I'm sending you these 'translations' of Sá Carneiro, because I would like to hear what you think of my somewhat free manner of anglicising them. The long piece is [...] effective I thought, and where I've altered it I'm not sure I've improved it. But the other two I changed – in detail – quite severely, as you'll see. I enjoyed doing these two so very much, so much so that if you would 'English' – roughly but as literally as possible (even to the word order), about a dozen, perhaps we could get a group ready for a magazine. But you might not like my verbal presumptions – though I'm sure the original looks much more bizarre. [...] The rougher & more literal the translations are the more suggestive to me they are. Just word by word transcription would be ideal.*[1]

Hughes, still fearing he was being too "free", admits that he had enjoyed tinkering with poems, but quickly adds that he is now willing to attempt a larger batch of translations no doubt in a less, as he thought, "self-indulgent" manner. In general, he preferred to work on batches rather than on individual poems; he was, in fact, opposed to publishing single examples of a poet's work and usually tried to secure many poems by the same author, believing that only exposure to a range of work might afford insight into a poet's imaginative world. Hughes defends himself against possible criticism, pleading that, presumptuous as the changes he has felt impelled to make might seem, he could still never hope to match the distinctiveness of the original. Immediately apparent, apart from his determination not to offend his collaborators, is a readiness to pay attention to suggestions from them and a willingness to receive their assessment of his efforts to make the foreign material accessible to *MPT*'s largely monoglot readership.

This is a remarkably unguarded communication, possibly because Hughes knew his interlocutors and could trust them not to take advantage of his openness. Projects based on friendship were at once attractive, but he was still uncertain as to how to proceed and was wary of simply allowing his own inclinations to guide him, as happened when translating the long poem "The Boy Changed into a Stag" by the Hungarian poet Ferenc Juhász, where he based his version on an existing poetic English version. Also noticeable is Hughes's optimism, at this time, vis-à-vis the literary world, his belief in the likelihood (not just possibility) of capturing its attention and engaging its support for his efforts.

With regard to Helder Macedo's own poetry, Hughes offers insight into his literary objectives when he writes:

First of all, about your poems, I like them very much, particularly the love poems ... I'm afraid I distorted your originals somewhat. Your poetry includes or indicates meanings that can't be nailed down with words, whereas the great characteristic (and great limitation) of my language is to nail things down. ... I feel I've spoiled the original to make a more concrete but less suggestive poem. ... [2]

In this instance, due to his long-standing friendship with Macedo, his interest in Portuguese poetry – especially that of Fernando Pessoa, whose work already had, in Jonathan Griffin, a distinguished translator – Hughes himself began to produce translations.

One might assemble a substantial anthology of occasional translations by Hughes, never evidently completed to his satisfaction, notably translation of poems by János Csokits. He also translated work by other friends, for example, Camillo Pennati, for some years in charge of the Italian Cultural Institute in London, who had translated some of Hughes's poetry into Italian. [3]

A significant project was Hughes's translation of poems by Lorenzo de

Medici, in collaboration with Italian informants. Since Lorenzo wrote in the more accessible Italian, one might suppose that Hughes was more able to connect with the source than was the case with Pilinszky and Hungarian. His co-translator, in this instance, was the writer and broadcaster Gaia Servadio, at the time in charge of programming at the Accademia Italiana in London. Servadio supplied Hughes with literal versions of a selection of poems, for a celebration of Lorenzo de Medici's poetry at the Accademia. Hughes, as usual, asked for versions that were more exact, presumably, than those he had first been offered. He explained, in a letter to Servadio, what he had in mind:

> *I had a go at the translation yesterday. After some hours, I got a pass-*
> *able version of that longish piece from the "altercazione"* [the verse
> exposition of Ficino's neo-Platonism, in which, incidentally, Hughes
> was greatly interested], *but remain uncertain about several details.*
> *Looking over the rest, I see many many more hours – not many more*
> *hours translating but many many more hours simply untangling the*
> *version to correspond with my guessing at the 15th century Italian, or*
> *even the plain Italian, of the original. If you could let me have an*
> *absolutely literal version – as primitive as you please, but literal (the*
> *more word by word literal the better) I fancy I could do it pretty*
> *quickly.*[4]

What is noteworthy here is his belief that it ought to be as easy for helpers to produce word-by-word versions as for him to finalize them. In fact this was not so, maybe because the conscientious providers of these texts felt it was, in a way, cheating or short-changing Hughes, not to supply commentary or interpretation as well, this seeming to be an intrinsic part of the assignment. Hughes soon became aware that what he was asking for was unusual and even potentially offensive since he needed texts that were not conventionally English texts, texts which might even be described as foreign-sounding. It was hard for Hughes's collaborators, he came to realize, to accept that he really did want word-for-word versions, even syntactically literal, what the Russians call *podstrochniki*, enabling the reader virtually to read the source text with the English mentally imprinted. There seems almost to be implied the naïve belief or wish that there was some way of shifting a poem bodily, as it were, from one language to another, with the translator functioning as a kind of mechanic. This was a radical view and easily misunderstood at a time when the crucial role of the translator was beginning to be recognized and at the same time subjected to simplification.

Hughes did collaborate with Servadio on the translation of poems by

Lorenzo de Medici, some eleven being completed and read at the Accademia celebration. Servadio had also read the poems to Hughes in the original language, while he urged her to let him know if there was anything in his translations that disturbed her. She commented on the difficulty of dealing with the many allusions to Dante, and recalls, at the same time, trying to interest Hughes in translating poems by Michelangelo, who had compared writing poetry to carving stone. This proposed collaboration, unfortunately, never took place.

Closer to home, Hughes also tried his hand at the translation of French poetry, though he did not particularly relish it. One of those invited to the first of the Poetry International readings in London in 1967 was Yves Bonnefoy, a leading French poet, essayist, art-historian and translator (of Shakespeare and Yeats). Anthony Rudolf, Bonnefoy's English translator, writes:

> I am inclined to think that Hughes started translating Bonnefoy for
> Poetry International, perhaps because he did not know of any other
> versions and then, doubtless having other priorities, ceded to me when
> he learnt of my translations. ... Another possibility is that Ted Hughes
> translated the poems for private reasons, in order to get to know them
> better. ... It is evident ... that Hughes had already embarked on his
> strategy of roughly/literal versions ...[5]

Bonnefoy was not the only French poet whose work Hughes attempted to translate. At one point he became involved in translating a selection of poems by Paul Eluard (1895-1952), as there appeared to be a likelihood of publication in the Penguin "Modern European Poets" series, the in-house editor at the time being Nikos Stangos. Hughes wrote to his sister:

> I have had a chance to translate Eluard for Penguin. I'm a bit reluctant
> to start on this translating lark, but I find it very easy to make quite
> close versions, quite good poetry, and if I had someone to check my
> French it might be worth it. ... I've read most of the Choix now, and
> roughly translated many of them.[6]

Hughes, in fact, produced some forty versions, and urged his sister to send him additional literal versions: "I want to qualify my sense of belonging to the English mentality as much as possible, and I would prefer to be mostly aware of any other capital's literary life than London's." Olwyn Hughes pointed out that it was Eluard in all probability who opened for Hughes the door to European poetry in general.

Hughes was sufficiently intrigued by the challenges posed by translation to respond positively to requests to contribute to various anthologies looking further afield than our own shores or America. He was among the first major British poets, not known also as a translator, to declare an interest in translation at that time. Nor was he averse to working with others, provided, as we have repeatedly seen, he could persuade them to provide him with what he called "word-by-word cribs". Stanley Kunitz, a senior American poet, once observed that he preferred working with a person like Max Hayward, with whom he collaborated on a selection of Anna Akhmatova's poetry, because it would take a lifetime to acquire the knowledge Hayward had at his fingertips. Hughes, who admired Kunitz's poetry, had a not dissimilar attitude; he greatly valued the collaboration of, for instance, János Csokits, to the point where he was convinced that the latter deserved at least as much credit for the final results as did he.

Hughes accepted an invitation from Bloodaxe Books to contribute translations of the contemporary Romanian poet Marin Sorescu (1936-1996), one of the most popular and widely translated poets of "the other Europe" and a frequent visitor to poetry festivals in Western Europe and elsewhere. His comments, in a letter of June 1986 to Edna Longley, who closely supervised the project, indicate his usual intention to remain as close to the literals he was sent as was grammatically and syntactically feasible, even expressing some doubts about making what might be regarded as essential changes to render the versions syntactically and grammatically normalized: "the literals you sent seem to me often just right. In several of these I've barely altered more than a word or two, as you'll see. I must say, my own feeling about translation is that I'm more and more interested in simply the literal cribs, with all their oddities." Evidently Hughes needed to feel he was in close contact with the source text and not merely glamorizing someone else's version.

V
Ovid's *Metamorphoses*
To Tell a Story

Probably Hughes's most admired and widely read translation is his selection of tales from Ovid's *Metamorphoses*. He had some linguistic grip on the text, presumably through his school Latin, and there was in addition the prose Loeb Classics translation by Frank Justus Miller (1858-1938), who had also translated Seneca's Tragedies, including *Oedipus*, a version used by Hughes and Peter Brook when the latter directed Seneca's *Oedipus* for the National Theatre.[1] Hughes also had recourse to the celebrated Arthur Golding Ovid translation of 1567 (Ezra Pound had called it one of the greatest poems in the English language).[2] One can assume that Hughes was particularly drawn to this, as Golding's was also the Ovid Shakespeare made use of, deriving from it, for example, his retelling of the "Salmacis and Hermaphroditus" episode.

Hughes was invited to contribute translations to a new version of episodes from *The Metamorphoses* and was, in fact, the most prolific contributor (four long sections) to this volume (1994), edited by Michael Hofmann and James Lasdun, who commissioned a number of contributions from American and British poets.[3] The editors allowed almost total latitude, explaining in their Introduction:

> *[W]e invited each contributor to translate, reinterpret, reflect on or complexly re-imagine the narrative. [...] We wanted an old remade, made new. By definition it resisted close control. Along the way, we decided ... to divide the book into self-contained narrative sections of anything from ten lines to ten pages, and to dispense with Ovid's division of the whole into individual books, while preserving his general running order as far as possible.*

They were clearly inviting a diversity of approaches and also encouraging contributors to be bold rather than timidly literalistic. Aware that in so dividing the work episodically, they were also disrupting the famous seamlessness of Ovid's narrative, they nevertheless decided on this strategy for practical reasons, and in the interest of freedom for the contributing poets, believing that readers would make the connections for themselves. There was some disappointment among Classicists that as a result of this strategy the links between the stories were no longer explicit; but there were gains, not least that the openness of the approach encouraged Hughes, for one, to continue translating Ovid.

In fact, Hughes continued to work on *Tales from Ovid: Twenty-four Passages from the Metamorphoses*.[4] He ends his introduction to his own selection, presented as separate episodes or poems, rather chillingly: "They establish a rough register of what it feels like to live in the psychological gulf that opens at the end of an era. Among everything else, we certainly recognize this." However, he vouchsafes nothing about his translation procedure, although it seems likely that he made use of Golding's translation, of the Latin source and Miller's prose version.

Shakespeare also drew on *The Metamorphoses* for his long poem "Venus and Adonis", discussion of which – and of Shakespeare's other long poem, "The Rape of Lucrece" – form the basis of Hughes's 1971 Introduction to his selection of poems from Shakespeare and later of his major scholarly enterprise *Shakespeare and the Goddess of Complete Being*.[5] As Hughes explains in his introduction to his selection of Shakespeare's verse, the key moment for tragedy shows "the agonies of an ancient Dionysus in a world of suddenly hardening sceptical intellect and morality ....In "Venus and Adonis", Venus, the love goddess, tries to rape Adonis, a severely puritan youth". The translation was also included in *Tales from Ovid*, as was the following one, "Salmacis and Hermaphroditus".

The significance of these poems for Hughes's own work cannot be exaggerated. In my selection of his translations (Faber, 2006), I accordingly, quote the entire "Venus and Adonis" section.[6] Hughes's may be described as a translation, insofar as he was guided by Ovid's vision. On the other hand, he modernized *The Metamorphoses*, as had Golding before him, and even Miller, although Ted Hughes's English is remoter from Miller's than from Golding's. That Ovid's retellings are enthralling stories is at once evident and Hughes, a resourceful narrator, successfully conveys their narrative vigour. Ezra Pound, as we have seen, refers to Golding's Ovid in the most positive terms, going so far as to ask: "Can we, for our part, know our Ovid if we do not find him in Golding?"[7] Furthermore, Pound insists that Golding has his eye firmly on the story and does not seek to "bemuse us with a rumble", that is, with his prosody. The same, surely, can be said of Hughes, who appreciated a good story when he heard it; his review of the Yiddish writer Isaac Bashevis

Singer's short stories, for instance, makes the point that Singer never introduced an inessential detail, everything being subordinated to the needs of the narration. The success of Hughes's *Ovid*, as of the original and of the Tudor translation, is surely due to his attention to the imperatives of story-telling.

An excerpt from "Salmacis and Hermaphroditus" will support this contention. The literalistic versions are followed by Golding's and Hughes's versions.

Prose version of this passage by Frank Justus Miller:

> *"I win, and he is mine!" cries the naiad, and casting off all her garments dives also into the waters: she holds him fast though he strives against her, steals reluctant kisses, fondles him, touches his unwilling breast, clings to him on this side and on that. At length, as he tries his best to break away from her, she wraps him round with her embrace, as a serpent, when the king of birds has caught her and is bearing her on high: which, hanging from his claws, wraps her folds about his head and feet and entangles his flapping wings with her tail: or as the ivy oft-times embraces great trunks of trees, or as the sea-polyp holds its enemy caught beneath the sea, its tentacles embracing him on every side.*

Line-by-line modern version by D.E. Hill:[8]

> *"I have won, and he is mine," cried out the Naiad, and she threw*
> *all her clothing well away from her and rushed into the middle of the*
> *waters*
> *and held him as he fought against her, violently snatching kisses*
> *and bringing her hands up under him and touching his unwilling*
> *breast;*
> *and now she draped herself around the youth this way and that.*
> *At last, though he struggled against her in his desire to get away,*
> *she entwined herself around him like a snake picked up by the king of*
> *birds*
> *and snatched aloft (as she hangs from him she binds his head*
> *and feet and entwines her tail around his spreading wings),*
> *or like ivy which likes to weave its way up tall tree trunks,*
> *or like an octopus catching and holding its enemy*

Golding:

The prize is won (cride Salmacis aloud) he is mine owne.
And therewithall in all post hast she having lightly throwne
Hir garments off, flew to the Poole and cast hir thereinto
And caught him fast between hir armes, for ought that he could doe:
Yea maugre all his wrestling and his struggling to and fro,
She held him still, and kissed him a hundred times and mo.
And willde he nillde he with hir handes she toucht his naked brest:
And now on this side now on that (for all he did resist
And strive to wrest him from hir gripes) she clung unto him fast:
And wound about him like a Snake which snatched up in hast
And being by the Prince of Birdes borne lightly up aloft,
Doth writhe hir selfe about his necke and griping talants oft:
And cast hir taile about his wings displayed in the winde:
Or like as Ivie runnes on trees about the utter rinde:
Or as the Crabfish having caught his enemy in the Seas,
Doth claspe him in on every side with all his crooked cleas.

Hughes:[9]

'I've won!' shrieked Salmacis. 'He's mine!'
She could not help herself.
'He's mine!' she laughed, and with a couple of bounds
Hit the pool stark naked
In a rocking crash and thump of water –
The slips of her raiment settling wherever
They happened to fall. Then out of the upheaval
Her arms reach and wind round him,
And slippery as the roots of big lilies
But far stronger, her legs below wind round him.
He flounders and goes under. All his strength
Fighting to get back up through a cloud of bubbles
Leaving him helpless to her burrowing kisses.
Burning for air, he can do nothing
As her hands hunt over him, and as her body
Knots itself every way around him
Like a sinewy otter

Hunting some kind of fish
That flees hither and thither inside him,
And as she flings and locks her coils
Around him like a snake
Around the neck and legs and wings of an eagle
That is trying to fly off with it,
And like ivy which first binds the branches
In its meshes, then pulls the whole tree down,
And as the octopus –
A tangle of constrictors, nippled with suckers,
That drag towards a maw –
Embraces its prey.

Vivid as Golding's lines are, Hughes's elaborations (for example, "slippery as the roots of big lilies"; "helpless to her burrowing kisses…"; "A tangle of constrictors, nippled with suckers") are as effective, as is his occasional use of contemporary diction (e.g., "Hit the pool stark naked…").

VI
Ferenc Juhász
History of a Translation

One of the first projects of *Modern Poetry in Translation* was for a Hungarian issue, to be guest-edited by János Csokits, including a selection of poems by Ferenc Juhász (b.1928), the inspiration, one might say, for this *MPT* project having been a poem by the latter called "The Boy Changed into a Stag Cries out at the Gate of Secrets". Hughes was impressed by the poem to such an extent that, on one occasion, when I was visiting him in Devon, primarily to discuss the projected Hungarian issue, he typed out a new version, based not on Juhász's Hungarian original, but on the Canadian poet Kenneth McRobbie's free English version.[1] This was the first and only time that he resorted to what must seem a dubious procedure, contradicting his principle of basing translations on verbally literal or close, un-mediated versions of the source text.

That Hughes was able to work in this unusually indirect manner was due to an affinity with the poem insofar as he was able to access it through another poet's version. Later, another Canadian poet, London-based at the time, David Wevill, produced a version of the same poem for a selection of Juhász's work, included in a Penguin "Modern European Poets" volume, alongside a selection (by Edwin Morgan) of poems by the acclaimed Sándor Weöres.[2] In his introduction to his Juhász versions, based on literals made for him by Flora Papastavrou, who also read the poems to him in the original language, Wevill, in similar terms to Auden, refers to the "Stag" as a great poem, rooted in Hungarian folklore. "The structure and rhythms of the poem", he adds, "derive to some extent from the regös-lays, the shaman-songs of ancient Hungary, where there is a magical creature called the Sun Stag…"

It is not hard to see why the poem should have appealed also to Hughes. While David Wevill's version is more immediately related to the source text, the Hughes version is close to being a distinctly different poem. Just how the version was produced by McRobbie, I do not know, but from the point of view of orthodox translation, Hughes's procedure seems problematical, the result nevertheless being a memorable poem. If the evolution of this hybrid work is not readily reconcilable with Hughes's own literalistic approach to translation, one must assume that he felt able, in this case, to indulge himself, if self-indulgence it be. (If Hughes was experimenting, it may have been because, in the context of an issue of a magazine, he felt under fewer constraints and able to take unusual liberties.)

In the latter case, however, one is bound to ask whether, left to his own devices, he might have produced more translations of this hybrid kind. My own belief is that the Juhász translation was a solitary, if spectacular, instance of a divergent approach. Arguably, of course, the self-imposed leash was simply too restrictive, which may also be why Hughes remarked to the Macedos that he had enjoyed taking liberties with some of the literal draft of Portuguese poetry they had sent him. It is also possible that, reworking McRobbie's version, feeling in tune with Juhász, he also felt he was somehow reinvesting the poem with something like its original inspiration or energy. If so, he had no grounds, beyond his own poetic intuition, for so thinking, and to my knowledge never again attempted anything of the like; but it is probably also true to say that he never again encountered a foreign poem that for him resonated so powerfully. In any event I do not think the occasion arose again, except, arguably, in connection with some of his theatre work, where he reworked classical dramas in an attempt to make them more stageworthy in modern terms.

It will be instructive to look at a passage of the Juhász translation, and at the McRobbie version on which it was based, as well as at David Wevill's version, which drew from literal texts by Flora Papastavrou. As mentioned, Ted Hughes had come across the Juhász poem in an anthology. While I was visiting him in Devon, he wrote his own version, translating at high speed. However, the issue for which it was intended was never produced, and I eventually returned the translation to Hughes. The whole text surfaced again when Hughes went through his papers before shipping them to Emory University, where I discovered it.[3]

The opening lines of the poem follows.

McRobbie version:

> Her own son the mother called
> from afar crying
> Her own son the mother called
> from afar crying,
> she went before the house, from there calling
> her hair's full knot she loosed,
> with it the dusk wove a dense quivering
> veil, a precious cloak down to her ankles...

Hughes:

> The mother called after her son
> From the far distance
> The mother called after her son
> from the far distance,
> she went out in front of the house, calling
> and she loosened her hair's thick knot
> which the dusk wove to a dense, stirring veil,
> a valuable robe sweeping the earth...

Wevill:

> The mother called to her own son,
> cried from far away,
> the mother called to her own son,
> cried from far away.
> went to the front of the house: from there she cried,
> unwound her heavy knot of hair
> dusk wove to a simmering bride's veil
> that flowed down to her ankles...

David Wevill wrote to me, explaining how his translation was produced:
Flora and I collaborated on Juhász, a kind of immersion process in which I was immersed in the Hungarian – sounds, rhythm, voice, etc. She worked with great patience and passion, and an ever-open dictionary (she was fluent, native, in fact, in the language) and should

have had equal billing in the translation. The subsoil of the versions was her... What I made into poems was material she provided me with, while making many choices, checking it against her knowledge – especially true of the complex "Stag" poem which is so unlike anything in English. She checked my versions closely and critically – it was, as I say, a collaboration, though the final poems were my responsibility and had to read as viable English poems. Flora's roughs were exhaustive and literal, some words had more than one meaning ... The grammars of the two languages are radically different, though in the parts about the mother crying out I think I kept some inversions, odd in English but somehow appropriate I felt, for rhythmic and musical effect, and to preserve the archaic, folkloric sense of the poem.

It would be inappropriate to comment in detail on the snippet of the poem I have provided, but I think it is fair to say that Hughes, as in the case of other translations when he was not working from source texts (e.g., his translations of Classical Greek and Roman drama), tried to energize the text, partly by somewhat normalizing the syntax and modernizing the diction (e.g., "from afar crying" becomes "From the far distance"). David Wevill, to a somewhat lesser extent, does likewise. Hughes brings into play his ability to visualize a scene sharply and, thus, his own descriptive powers. However, it also seems to me that he is not aiming fully to naturalize his text. Indeed, he demonstrably "foreignizes", even if not translating directly or indirectly from the source. Again, Wevill does likewise. It should be pointed out that both translators were taking a risk, as in general there was little appreciation of such tactics at the time. Both poets are also concerned that their co-workers should receive equal credit.

Since this is the only occasion, as far as I know, in which Ted Hughes produced a text of this hybrid kind, it cannot be categorized in terms of his own work. Nevertheless, arguably, the final product belongs almost as much among his own poems as among his translations.

My purpose, however, has been to show that Hughes was not bound by rigid codes of translation theory, but was prepared, when the occasion demanded, to produce versions based on a less than ideal acquaintance with the source. However, even here he comes to terms with the work in question at a more basic level, and, one must suppose, was able by now to use his experience of translation and the ways of interpreters, to intuit what was embodied in the original.

VII

Phèdre, The Oresteia
Metre and Grandiloquence

Robert Lowell's Preface to his translation of one of Racine's masterpieces, *Phèdre*, is a modest piece, in which he identifies certain problems to do with translation and despairs of finding a solution. He concludes: "I have translated as a poet and tried to give my lines a certain dignity, speed, and flare... The syllabic Alexandrines do not and cannot exist in English." He points out that, even so, he does not ignore the metre and tries to convey the formal quality of the text by maintaining an iambic line and rhymed couplets, though he adds self-depreciatingly, "I have been tormented by the fraudulence of my heavy touch."[1]

Hughes, a less formal poet than Lowell, was more moved by the myth itself than by Racine's measured treatment of it. Lowell notes that his own metre is based on Dryden and Pope and laments the fact that neither of these poets attempted to work with Racine, whereas they lavished much attention on the more "inaccessible" Homer and Virgil. He points out that although he himself has aimed at an idiomatic style, he inevitably echoes the English of the Restoration. His own work, he adds finally, lacks the "diamond edge" of Racine, who uses a smaller vocabulary than any English poet. Racine's greatness lies in "the justness of rhythm and logic, and the glory of his hard, electric rage". Some of the qualities that Lowell sees in the original, he has, nevertheless, captured and it is arguably because he has been so fascinated by them that he was drawn to translating Racine in the first place.

Ted Hughes decides from the start that he will not attempt to reproduce or imitate Racine's metre by means of formal English verse. Like Lowell, however, he exploits his own strengths as a writer and, also like Lowell, translates *Phèdre* "as a poet", with his talent for graphically incisive English. It should be remembered that his previous experience of translating plays had been with Peter Brook and the production of Seneca's *Oedipus*. Theseus, too, in *Phèdre*, is a more than life-size Greek hero of dubious morals, a dallier with women, a man too impulsive for his own good. The outcome is as, or more, disastrous and in this case the hero is no longer Theseus nor "Hippolytus" but Queen Phaedra herself. It seems that Hughes's principal concern was to retell the story with immediacy and to maintain as unwavering a focus on the queen herself as does Racine or Euripides in his *Hippolytus*.

Jean Racine (1639-1699) was born into a religious family, associated with Port Royal, the centre of Jansenism, and was educated at the Jansenist College in Beauvais. With the success of his play *Andromaque* in 1667, Racine's talent became obvious. Ted Hughes's version of *Phèdre* was first performed, in London, by the Almeida Theatre Company in August 1998. There was an earlier version, as we have seen, by Robert Lowell, who also wrote a staged version of *The Oresteia*.[2]

The main problem, as noted, has to do with Racine's use of Alexandrines, the French heroic meter, which has no proper equivalent in the English tradition, though attempts have been made to imitate it by means of heroic metre, iambic pentameter (in rhyming couplets). In the preface to his *Phaedra*, Lowell talks of basing his metre on Dryden's and Pope's, but running his couplets on and avoiding inversions and alliterations. He regrets, as we have seen, that he inevitably echoes the style of the English Restoration. Tony Harrison later (1975) distances himself still further, transposing the play into an episode of British rule in India before the 1857 Mutiny.[3] Hughes reshapes the play in terms of contemporary theatre, but otherwise remains as close as possible to the source text. Blank verse, the obvious option, did not seem viable. Implicitly he recognized the limits of translation, and aimed to convey Racine's masterpiece as human drama rather than in its literary-historical context.

Hughes was interested in Greek drama and seems not to have been too fussy about the form in which it came to him, via Seneca's Latin version or, still further removed, via Racine's seventeenth-century French. One may speculate as to what it was about *Phèdre* that attracted Hughes. An examination of his papers at Emory, however, has revealed no commentary by him such as exists in connection with his version of Seneca's *Oedipus*, though he did preserve the drafts of his *Phèdre*, so that it becomes possible to follow the translation process itself.

Hughes did not return to Classical drama until much later in his life, with *Alcestis*, a myth which, it seems likely, fascinated him for personal reasons. In his translation of Aeschylus' *Oresteia*, as in the Seneca and Racine translations, he does not attempt to reproduce the metre, but seeks to confront the myth head on. However, he also exercises self-restraint, true to his "literalistic" ideals, so that if or when he takes liberties, these are in the form of deletion rather than addition or invention. While aiming at immediacy, Hughes is not unmindful of formal considerations. There are other versions, including not only that by Lowell, but also a much earlier, radically foreignizing one by none other than Robert Browning.

Lowell preceded Hughes with a rhyming version of Racine's *Phèdre*, his foreword to the translation of Aeschylus relevant also in the present context:

> *I do not want to cry down my translation of Aeschylus, but to say what I've tried to do and not tried. I have written from other translations, and not from the Greek. One in particular, Richmond Lattimore's, has had my admiration for years; it is so elaborately exact. I have aimed at something else: to trim, cut, and be direct enough to satisfy my own mind and at a first hearing the simple ears of a theatre audience.[5]*

Lowell, justly no doubt – unlike Hughes he had studied the Greek source text – stresses the virtual impossibility of representing the *Oresteia* in contemporary English. His commendation of Lattimore's "elaborately exact"version would have caught Ted Hughes's eye and one may assume that Hughes also consulted Lattimore in his attempt to establish a sense of the otherwise inscrutable source text. [6]

It is not known what Hughes's sources were, although it seems probable that he made use of the Vellacott Penguin translation of the Oresteian Trilogy. Hughes first offered the play to the Northcott Theatre in Exeter, and the National Theatre production was commissioned for performance in the autumn of 1999, the year following Ted Hughes's death. This production lacked discussion with the translator-author, and some of its evidently up-to-date political references might not have appealed to him.

A comparison of several versions will illustrate what Ted Hughes hoped to achieve. Below is a passage from the opening speech of the Watchman, who has been waiting for news from Troy and who now announces the triumphant return of King Agamemnon.

A recent scholarly version by Hugh Lloyd-Jones of this opening passage:[7]

> *I have power to tell of the auspicious command of the*
> *expedition, the command of men*
> *in authority; for still from the gods am I inspired*
> *with persuasive power, my strength in song, by the life that has*
> *grown up with me:*

69

To tell how the two-throned command of the Achaeans, of the
 youth of Hellas
the concordant leadership,
was sped with avenging spear and arm
by the warlike bird of omen to the Teucrian land,
the king of birds appearing to the kings of the ships,
the black eagle and behind it the white one,
appearing near the palace on the hand in which the spear is
brandished,
in seats conspicuous,
feeding upon the hare, her womb teeming with young,
checked from running her final course.
...

Robert Lowell, from *Agamemnon, Part One of The Oresteia*:[8]

I know the omen of the angry birds
Hurled Agamemnon and Menelaus
like a spear at Troy – two thrones, one mind!
Two eagles came to our kings,
one white-tailed, the other black.
They lit on the spear-hand side of the palace.
Everyone saw them. They killed a hare.
Her unborn young were bursting from her side.

Richmond Lattimore, from *The Agamemnon of Aeschylus*:

I have mastery yet to chant the wonder at the wayside
given to kings. Still by god's grace there surges within me
singing magic
grown to my life and power,
how the wild bird portent
hurled forth the Achaeans'
twin-stemmed power single hearted,
lords of the youth of Hellas,
with spear and hand of strength
to the land of Teucrus.
Kings of birds to the kings of the ships,

one black, one blazed with silver,
clear seen by the royal house
on the right, the spear hand,
they lighted, watched by all
tore a hare, ripe, bursting with young unborn yet,
stayed from her last fleet running.
Sing sorry, sorrow: but good wins out in the end.

Ted Hughes, from *The Oresteia: A new version by Ted Hughes*:

I'm sick of the heavens, sick of the darkness.
The one light I wait for never comes.
Maybe it never will come –
A beacon-flare that leaps from peak to peak
Bringing the news from Troy –
"Victory! After ten years, Victory!"
The one word that Clytemnestra prays for.
Queen Clytemnestra – who wears
A man's heart in a woman's body,
A man's dreadful will in the scabbard of her body
Like a polished blade. A hidden blade
Clytemnestra reigns over fear.
I get up sodden with dew.
I walk about, to shift my aches.
I lie down – the aches harden worse.
No dreams. No sleep. Only fear –
Fear like a solid lump of indigestion
Here, high in my belly – a seething.
Singing's good for fear
But when I try to sing – weeping comes.
I weep. There's no keeping it down.
Everything's changed in this palace.
The old days,
The rightful King, order, safety, splendour,
A splendour that lifted the heart –
All gone,
You Gods,
Release me.

Hughes, visualizing the scene as myth, as well as in contemporary terms, is able to update or personalize, without altering the ritual nature of the original and transports himself into the body of the Watchman, describing not just what he sees but what he feels as well. For Hughes, it seems, the myth is alive, as it must have been for Aeschylus. Hughes calls on his imagination and sense of stage-worthiness, and does not attempt to reproduce, at least literally, the formal qualities of the source text, an endeavour which evidently preoccupied Lowell, and the lack of which in Hughes was criticized by Classical scholars, or critics of his treatment, who felt that the translator had imposed on Aeschylus Ted Hughes's own sense of the meaning of the Oresteian tragedy. Hughes does, however, make use of his ability to convey the power of the Oresteian story, and at key moments – the play opens with one of these – his touch is evident. He allows his language to become almost contemporary and therefore subject to dating; while one can see what Browning had in mind, in this regard, Browning's version is no longer alive for us, and Hughes's translation, too, may already be moving linguistically out of range. Still, it seems to me that there is a minimal amount in the Hughes version subject to this process of attrition, and much that remains as vivid as when he wrote it. In any case, it is current in terms of his own work.

Racine's *Phèdre*, unlike the English translation, is divided into scenes and in the following speech of Phèdre, opening Scene 2, the queen addresses her nurse Oenone.

N'allons point plus avant, demeurons, chère Oenone.
Je ne me soutiens plus; ma force m'abandonne:
Mes yeux sont éblouis du jour que je revoi;
Et mes genoux tremblants se dérobent sous moi.
Hélas!

Hughes translates this as follows:

No further, Oenone. I stop here.
That last scrap of strength has left me suddenly.
I can't stay upright and I need not try.
The sun's light is too painful.
My wretched, trembling legs have gone numb.

He has substituted "have gone numb" for "cannot support me" in the last line, making the passage more idiomatic. From the start, Hughes is not concerned with attempting to produce a facsimile, as it were, of the stately French text; indeed, it is hard to see how this could have been done without considerable paraphrase or the invention of a purpose-constructed English equivalent to the Alexandrine, or by use of the heroic metre employed by Pope in his Homer translation, which might have necessitated much manipulation of the text. Hughes chose instead to adhere to the source text, but attempts to produce an idiomatically playable English script. Thus, he adds, in line 3, "and I need not try" and reduces or concentrates line 4, in Racine's (lit.) "My eyes are dazzled by the day which I see again" to "the sun's light is too painful". Line 5 is a more-than-usually free translation or interpretation of the French "My knees trembling give way under me..." Clearly aware of the inevitable loss in resonance, Hughes tries at least to preserve the dramatic impact of the original.

But how does Lowell handle these lines?

> *Dearest, we'll go no further. I must rest.*
> *I'll sit here. My emotions shake my breast,*
> *The sunlight throws black bars across my eyes.*
> *My knees give. If I fall, why should I rise...*

Lowell has substituted iambic pentameter couplets for Racine's Alexandrines, also reproducing the rhymes. "Dearest" is a free translation, presumably, of "chère Oenone". In line 3, Lowell seeks to energize the French line, assisting it with his own notion of what is metaphorically effective. Although Hughes "takes liberties", he does not attempt to invigorate the text in this direct way. Lowell has made an effort to convey or reproduce the formal grandeur of the Alexandrine lines, whereas Hughes is principally concerned with writing a playable text while retaining the context of the myth. That is, he has not tried to render linguistic aspects of Racine's text, making two changes, in this short speech, eliminating line 3 as redundant and in order to juxtapose line 2 more immediately with the line about the sun, while making a substitution in line 5 to bring his text closer to the French, which tells of Phèdre's knees giving way under her.

Act One closes with these lines spoken by Phèdre, again addressing Oenone:

Eh bien! A tes conseils je me laisse entrainer.
Vivons, si vers la vie on peut me ramener,
Et si l'amour d'un fils, en ce moment funeste,
De mes faibles esprit peut ranimer le reste.

Hughes:

Yes, yes, yes, your words are only too clear.
Now let me live – if that be possible.
Can mother love be strong enough
To revive what's left of my spirit?

The last two lines above were deleted by Hughes in the copy he gave me and the following, with fewer Freudian associations, substituted:

Let my love for my son be strong enough
To revive what's left of my spirit.

Lowell:

So be it! Your superior force has won.
I will live if compassion for my son,
Devotion to the Prince, and love of power
Can give me courage in this fearful hour.

A certain resonance, this being the conclusion of an Act, was probably felt by Lowell to be necessary, which may also be why Hughes decides not to end with a question. Lowell, who has maintained rhyming couplets throughout, is arguably better placed to end on a resonant note. Again Hughes seems to have opted, rather, for lines which may be spoken without risk of melodrama. Lowell has drawn attention to the historico-political aspect of this speech with his reference to "the Prince" (not in the French text), whereas Hughes, here as elsewhere, focuses on the human, it being at least doubtful that the political connotations, familiar to the audience of the time, will still pertain.

A more literal version by John Cairncross maintains a regular metre and aims at a certain resonance, reading:[9]

Then be it so. Your counsels have prevailed.
I'll live, if I can be recalled to life,
And if the love I bear my son can still
In this grim hour revive my failing strength.

Hughes seems not to have been influenced by this, although he probably also referred to Cairncross's widely available translation as yet another guide to the sense. He has concentrated instead on making the language credible in terms of contemporaneity. This is not to denigrate other approaches but merely to suggest Hughes's priorities.

If one views this translation in the context of Hughes's development as a poet, one is above all impressed by the problem it sets of how to convey passion, the irony and cruelty of a seemingly irreversible fate, via formal verse. Hughes is the product of an era in which traditional form was accorded much respect. He had admired Robert Graves's poetry and himself been influenced in his early poetry by the formally rigorous American poet, John Crowe Ransom. While surely conscious of Racine's formalities, he was committed, as we have seen, to reproduce, instead, the text semantically, and to find an appropriate English for it, not strictly informal but not conventionally formal either. As with T.S. Eliot in his plays, Hughes was searching for a flexible language concentratedly to convey passions that could not be expressed in the language of ordinary discourse; and yet the discourse, to be effective on the stage, had also to partake of the ordinary. Hughes's conveys the text economically, while eschewing the obvious formalities that Racine, or even Lowell, had deployed, which might have rendered it virtually unplayable.

Ted Hughes had a good sense of theatre, and was particularly aware of the need to maintain pace or continuity. His version of *Phèdre* energetically conveys the mythic content. He accomplishes this by attending to the means by which the source text had also achieved its effects. Hughes was an accomplished story-teller, focusing on the story itself, especially with regard to his theatrical work, where the need to retain the audience's attention was paramount. That he succeeded is attributable surely to the acumen with which he was able to reimagine the myth itself. This is noticeable, above all, in the totality, the overall conception, the result also of a collaborative effort between director, cast, and translator-writer. It is unlikely that we shall ever know how or to what extent Hughes's version was influenced by the input of actors, but this must have been a reciprocal process and he certainly remained open to suggestions from those immediately involved, Hughes's theatrical apprenticeship after all having been with Peter Brook, who stresses the importance of the insight of actors.

A look at one passage will, I hope, highlight Hughes's methods. Since he was in the habit of preserving his notes and drafts, it is possible, even in the absence of any self-commentary, to obtain a sense of his approach.

Act Two: Hippolytus makes a declaration of love to Aricia. Below is part of his declaration, the French text first:

Présent je vous fuis; absente, je vous retrouve;
Dans le fond de forêts votre image me suit;
La lumière du jour les ombres de la nuit,
Tout retrace à mes yeux les charmes que j'évite;
Tout vous livre à l'envi le rebelle Hippolyte.
Moi-même, pour tout fruit de mes soins superflus,
Maintenant je me cherche, et ne me trouve plus;
Mon arc, mes javelots, mon char, tout m'importune;
Je ne me souviens plus les leçons de Neptune:
Mes seuls gémissements font retentir les bois,
Et mes coursiers oisifs ont oublié ma voix,
Peut-être le récit d'un amour si sauvage
Vous fait, en m'écoutant, rougir de votre ouvrage.

Ad-verbum version:
Present, I escape you; absent, I discover you;
In the depth of the forest your image pursues me;
The light of day, the shadows of night,
Reiterate the charms I am trying to avoid;
Everything makes you desirable to rebellious Hippolytus.
Myself, the sole fruit of my superfluous labour,
I seek now and no longer find;
My bow, my javelins, my chariot, all embarrass me;
I no longer recall the lessons of Neptune:
Only my moans echo in the woods,
And my idle horses have forgotten my voice,
Perhaps my declaration of this untutored love
Will make you, listening to me, blush at what you have done.

Hughes:
I search your absence for you like a madman,
And yet I run from your presence.
Everywhere in the woods your image hunts me,
I try to escape you
But every shaft of sunlight,

Every night shadow
Sets you in front of me, surrounds me with you.
Everything competes to fling
The obstinate fool Hippolytus
Helpless at your feet.
All my studied care to preserve myself
Has brought me to this – I have lost myself,
I search – but I cannot find myself,
My bow, my spears, my chariot,
They beckon to me, I ignore them.
The breaking and taming of wild horses,
Everything the god of the sea taught me,
It is beyond me – I have forgotten it.
My own horses run wild –
They have forgotten my voice.
Nothing hears my voice but the forest –
The black, echoing depth of the forest.
Yes, my love is a savage.
What raving words these are!
Maybe you blush to hear them.

VIII
The Tibetan Book of the Dead
An Oratorio

From early days, Ted Hughes had taken an interest in the *Bardo Thödol*, *The Tibetan Book of the Dead*, a text he came across in America when he and Sylvia Plath spent Autumn 1959 in the artists' colony in Yaddo, Saratoga Springs, although he had also encountered it as a student in Cambridge in the early 1950s, and had even discussed it with his American friend and Cambridge contemporary Lucas Myers. At Yaddo, Hughes was working on *Lupercal*,[1] his second poetry collection, and met the Chinese-American composer Chou Wen-Chung, who invited him to write a libretto for an opera he was planning, based on the ancient Tibetan book.[2]

Hughes thus describes the *Bardo*:

> [T]he geography and furnishings of the afterworld are Buddhist, but the main business of the work as a whole, which is to guide a dead soul to its place in death, or back into life – together with the principal terrific events, and the flying accompaniment of descriptive songs, exhortation to the soul, threats, and the rest – are all characteristically shamanic. This huge, formal work has long ago lost contact with any shaman, but its origins seem clear.[3]

He later linked this to the poetic temperament we call 'romantic' and to Shakespeare's *Venus and Adonis* (itself a key to his own interpretation of the Shakespeare work), Yeats's *The Wanderings of Oisin*, Eliot's *Ash Wednesday*, and also to myths such as those of Orpheus and Herakles and epics such as *Gilgamesh* (a stage representation of which he also sketched) and *The Odyssey* (a passage of which he translated, on commission from the BBC).

The *Bardo* text was put into written form by the legendary Padma Sambhava in the 8th century AD, "*Bardo Thödol*" meaning "liberation by hearing on the after-death plane", and the book is indeed a practical guide for the dead during the state held to intervene between death and the next rebirth. It was traditionally read aloud to the dying to help in the attainment of liberation, encouraging use of the moment of death to recognize the nature of mind and to reach liberation, seeking to persuade the dying and even the deceased that the peaceful and terrifying wrathful visions appearing are gathered karma, self-generated, *The Tibetan Book of the Dead* teaching how to achieve or earn liberation from the endless cycle of birth and rebirth, cyclic suffering.

Professor Chou Wen-Chung relates how there was considerable interaction between Hughes and himself over quite a long period. The work, "for musical and staging reasons", could not, in his view, really be regarded as a translation. But, as we have seen, this kind of hybrid production was not unusual for Hughes, to the extent that his involvement with translation impels one to re-draw the latter's boundaries. Here, because of the complexity of the source material, a good deal of condensing was necessary. The composer confirms that the text used by Hughes was the Evans-Wentz translation, which it is possible was introduced to him by Chou himself, although it also seems possible that Hughes had already encountered it in Cambridge some years before meeting Chou, who observes that: "[Hughes] had already done some work on the *Bardo*". Not surprisingly for such a large-scale project it continued to gestate throughout his creative life, since he was contemplating a return to it shortly before his death, being sufficiently interested to write to Chou, proposing that they resume work, even after so much time had elapsed. Although the latter, according to Lucas Myers, who queried Professor Chou specifically about it, expressed his willingness, the project was not resumed, so that the Hughes text is unchanged from the original 1959 draft.

In general, Hughes's views on translation, what he regarded as legitimate in relation to pre-existing works, were constrained. However, he was hardly bound even by considerations of genre and thus was able to collaborate with composers, doing so on at least one other occasion; this was his work on *Vasco*, in part a translation of the French anti-war drama, *Histoire de Vasco* (1957) by the Lebanese-born playwright Georges Schehadé (1905-1989). Commissioned by the Sadler's Wells Opera Company, with music by Gordon Crosse, this was a full-scale opera in three acts for seventeen solo voices, chorus and orchestra.[4] Hughes was not averse to such collaborations, indeed appears to have welcomed them, perhaps because he was on the lookout for ways of circumventing the ever-ready negative response to high art. In 1979, Faber published Hughes's sequence of poems *Remains of Elmet*, which gave equal billing to Fay Godwin, whose photographs had inspired Hughes's writing.[5]

Hughes devoted some six months to work on the *Bardo* text and it seems to have prompted or at least to have been among the promptings for a number of original works by him (in particular his third book, *Wodwo*, 1967).[6] In a radio interview he remarks, in a disarmingly casual manner, of his radio play *The Wound*, included in *Wodwo*:

> Well it was a freak production really. At the time I was writing a sce-
> nario of the Bardo Thödol – Tibetan Book of the Dead [...] and at the
> end of it I had a dream, which was the dream of 'The Wound'... much,
> much more complicated than the play as it is now... Well it was just like
> a full-length play, with many scenes, many things going on, but along
> with it was a full text. So I dreamed the action of the play, and was in
> the play, but simultaneously dreamed a very full text. And came out of
> the dream and woke up – and in the dream, this play had been written
> by John Arden.[7]

Particularly interesting is the interplay of dream or shamanic vision and ambition, evidence that the project related to significant concerns; the dreamed part relating specifically to Hughes's practical considerations, even to his interest in John Arden's play *Serjeant Musgrave's Dance*. Hughes comments on the play and on his dream: "I interpreted it first of all as a sort of Celtic *Bardo Thödol* – a Gothic *Bardo Thödol* – because, in fact, it's full of all the stock imagery of a journey to the Celtic underworld..." Again, he offers insight into the origins of his version of the *Bardo* and its connection with his work in general, especially with regard to his interest in the shamanic journey, which, among other aspects of Shamanism, he discusses in a review of Mircea Eliade's *Shamanism*, 1964.[8]

Translation for Hughes, thus, might be either adaptation, based on engagement with the text, or, more clearly, what he liked to think of as literalistic or word-by-word, where his model was nearer to W.H.I. Bleek's anthropological transcriptions and translations of Bushman folklore. To anticipate a little, these apparently somewhat divergent aims combined in Hughes's later adaptations of Classical Greek drama (*Oresteia* and *Alcestis*).[9] With the *Bardo* text, possibly because Hughes was participating in a joint project, and also because the material was culturally remote, his work may be characterized as relating to and involving translation, rather than as constituting translation as such. What he achieved may, in fact be better viewed as original work, even if owing its inception to pre-existing texts as to his own preoccupations, and discussions with others (e.g., in the case of the *Bardo*, his discussions with Lucas Myers, who had a deep interest in Buddhism).

Just as one cannot adequately assess Pope's poetic achievements without taking into account his translation of the Homeric epic, the *Bardo* oratorio should surely be included among Hughes's own work or original writings. Obviously translation and so-called original writing are not so distinct as they at first seem, even if some readers felt that Hughes had been hamstrung by his concern for literal accuracy, ignoring that he *deliberately* eschewed the path of "imitation", though this was more likely to win him acclaim. That the *Bardo* oratorio has not so far been included among Hughes's original writings may also be because it was never completed, which is to say that it did not result in an actual production.

The *Bardo* project was not the only operatic one in Hughes's career. I have mentioned his version of Georges Schehadé's *Histoire de Vasco*. Along with Ionesco, Adamov and Beckett, Schehadé, who began his literary career as a poet, is regarded as one of the originators of the "New Theatre" of the 1950s; significantly, perhaps, Schehadé himself has referred to the "New Theatre" as a "Theatre of Poetry", the *Histoire de Vasco* (1957) being described as a fantasy comedy, with one foot in a Ruritanian setting at the start of the century and the other in contemporary military realities having to do with the Algerian War. Vasco, the eponymous hero, is a Chaplinesque figure, a humble yet courageous *homme moyen universel*. The drama unfolds in a series of scenes or tableaux which lend themselves to poetic treatment. In this case, Hughes's work on *Vasco* did result in an actual production. Nevertheless, the *Bardo* project was more significant for him, its complexity being among the circumstances accounting no doubt for its never being fully realized, although Hughes's draft version is virtually complete. He might have revised it in rehearsal, as he did with his very late version of *Phèdre*. What remains is perhaps best seen as a reading, rather than a final performance-text.

The *Bardo* oratorio, as evidenced by Hughes's desire so late in his career and life to return to it, seems to have been one of particular significance, relating to his interest in Shamanism. The oratorio represents a direct engagement with the text of *The Tibetan Book of the Dead* into which Hughes imports almost verbatim a number of passages connected with ritualistic invocations.

Interestingly, Jung wrote an introduction, described as a "psychological commentary", to the Evans-Wentz edition of the *Bardo Thödol*. It is likely that it was this essay that directed Ted Hughes's attention to the Swiss psychiatrist and his writings. Lucas Myers also relates Hughes's absorption in the *Bardo* to an earlier piece, the radio play, *The Wound*, where his protagonist,

Ripley, is the original of the protagonist in Hughes's short story "Difficulties of a Bridegroom". Although the *Bardo* oratorio is closer to the source text in some places, Myers believes that Hughes's own ideas, too, are reflected in it. This seems likely, as no major translation or translation project undertaken by Hughes was ever casual. In his memoir of Ted Hughes and Sylvia Plath, Myers cites a letter by Hughes in which he comments that "in the middle ages vision was a common way of thinking, a kind of controlled dreaming awake", adding that "now we are so stupidly self-conscious that this perfectly commonplace gift has hidden itself completely."[10]

So, how should the *Bardo* oratorio be described, since a plain translation it is not? Perhaps it is best regarded as an adaptation, closely related to other concerns of Hughes, to be read in the context of these, rather than as simply reflecting curiosity about an exotic cultural monument. Hughes borrowed freely from the Evans-Wentz translation, but the work was also influenced by his own interests. In the case of the *Bardo* oratorio and also of Classical Greek or Latin plays, he was more concerned with producing playable texts than translations to be judged by standards of academic accuracy. When dealing with texts that had received much attention and of which scholarly and other editions existed, he evidently did not feel it incumbent to produce scholarly precise versions, but allowed himself to become more personally involved. The *Bardo* is among these latter productions, and indeed prepares the ground for what follows.

The Tibetan Book of the Dead oratorio, taking advantage of the circumstances which had brought him into contact with the composer, was a project that engaged Hughes's attention at Yaddo and later even distracted him from his own poetry, namely his second volume, *Lupercal*. As shown, there was a background to his engagement with the *Bardo* project, and the library at Yaddo provided him with texts that he first encountered in the Cambridge University Library, including the Evans-Wentz translation of the Tibetan source text. Since, however, he did also complete work on *Lupercal*, it appears that the *Bardo* project was stimulating rather than distracting; it is even arguable that he needed to be working on a variety of contrasting if related projects. In the case of the *Bardo*, I believe he was concerned with producing a text, the public performance of which might render an esoteric document more generally accessible. So concerned was he indeed, that he attempted to re-engage with this project near the end of his life.

Hughes's attitude to translation, or the use made of it, was thus not limited to what is generally understood by the term, varying from versions of literalism to adaptations, as in his work on *The Tibetan Book of the Dead*. However, a comparison of some passages in his version of the Evans-Wentz translation shows that he attempted to adhere to the latter's scholarly renderings, assumed to be accurate, at least at key points. He did not have direct access to the source text, but his interest in Tibetan Buddhism enabled him to render this material more audible, by embodying it in a work that envisaged a spectacular performance – even if this did not result from his collaboration with Chou.

Still, one wonders how he reconciled this freer approach with generally literalistic aims. Maybe he made a distinction between his work on the oratorio and his work with, say, the poetry of Pilinszky or Amichai, where he was in personal contact with the authors and, to some extent, shared their historical experience, though with the Tibetan text there was also a nexus of connections, touching on his interest in the work of Jung. It is, perhaps, also worth noting that the therapeutic value of art was of perennial concern to him. In his work on the *Bardo*, he was of course dealing with death directly, this being particularly relevant when he seemed to be approaching the end of his own life.

His anthropological studies as a student in Cambridge prepared him to some extent for this work, but he was in any case temperamentally inclined to consider life *sub specie aeternitatis*. When he suggested to the composer that they resume work, it was not so much timely as already too late.

It is also not too much to claim that, in his open-mindedness and with his pedagogical ambitions, Hughes was himself looking for ways of making what he regarded as essential messages more generally accessible; hence his Blakeian impatience at the failure of the educational system to encourage the life of the imagination, and his interest in educational reform, evidenced in such works as his friends C.B. Cox's and A.E. Dyson's *The Black Papers on Education*.[11] Various other bold initiatives, such as the Sacred Earth Drama Trust, of which Hughes was a trustee, engaged him, and he was involved in campaigns to safeguard the environment, a striking example of his activism being his poem "The Black Rhino", included in his last book, *Wolfwatching* (1989). He used the visibility of his post as British Poet Laureate to provide these projects with a public platform.

Though Hughes based his *Bardo* text largely on the Evans-Wentz translation, he permitted himself to depart from the primary translator's wording. Thus, his description of the process of death has apparently no direct connection with the translation, while the prayer to the Buddhas and Bodhisattvas draws on the prayers or "Paths of Good Wishes", given as an appendix to the Evans-Wentz volume. Here is an excerpt from the translation, on which Hughes drew to produce his own composite version of the prayers:

> *O ye Compassionate Ones, ye possess the wisdom of understanding, the love of compassion, the power of [doing] divine deeds and of protecting, in incomprehensible measure. Ye Compassionate Ones such-and-such a person is passing from this world to the world beyond. He is leaving this world. He is taking a great leap...*"

Hughes's draft of the "Obeisances" reads:

> *To the Divine Body of Truth, the Incomprehensible,*
> > *Boundless Light;*
> *To the Divine Body of Perfect Endowment, Who are the*
> > *Lotus and the Peaceful and the Wrathful Deities;*
> *To the Lotus-born Incarnation, Padma Sambhava, Who is*
> > *the Protector of all sentient beings;*
> *To the Gurus, the Three Bodies, obeisance.*

The process seems distinct from Hughes's literalistic dependence, for instance, on János Csokits's English versions of Pilinszky or on Yehuda Amichai's English renderings of his own poems. Hughes was never a slave to theory nor bound by notions of consistency. Since, as far as I know, there is no written record of his collaboration with Professor Chou on the *Bardo* oratorio, we cannot guess what the process was. Although Hughes's work on the *Bardo* occurred very early in his career, before his more systematic engagement with this form of writing, his interest in the ancient Tibetan manual predated his fortuitous meeting with Chou at Yaddo, which must have seemed an opportunity to pursue an earlier interest in Buddhism and Shamanism. The resulting work, as noted, is an example of a text largely dependent *on* rather than *constituting* translation; it is perhaps to be located *between* translation and original writing.

 To return to what he wrote in a review of Mircea Eliade's *Shamanism*: "The geography and furnishings of the after-world are Buddhist, but the main business of the work [...] are all characteristically shamanic." Hughes makes connections across culture, genre, historical epoch, so that his work must be read seamlessly if the intellectual elements and the roots of his motivation are to be perceived. Where possible, he sought, as in a later but long-pondered work (*Shakespeare or the Goddess of Complete Being*, 1992), systematically to supply his vision with a basis in fact. It is hardly likely, therefore, that he would have subscribed to a single translational approach, but it is also clear that for him the path followed by Robert Lowell was not one to be replicated. For one thing, like his *Wodwo* (see the title and last poem in *Wodwo*, 1967: "What am I? Nosing here, turning leaves over / Following the faint stain on the air of the river's edge..."), Hughes was far too curious, his attention being directed outward, as was, for instance, that of Arthur Golding, the Tudor translator of Ovid's *Metamorphoses*.

IX
Peter Brook, Drama as Paradigm
Seneca's *Oedipus*

Although his early work was remarkable, Ted Hughes made his most important contribution as a translator in his later years. He regarded writing for the theatre as of major significance, not only because the theatre engaged the interest of a far larger public, but also because writing for it, he felt, was therapeutic; to his friends he often recommended writing plays, as a means of identifying different sides of the self, allocating parts to characters and observing how they fared in interaction with one another, a practical strategy, he believed, for dealing with problems. In his introduction to Amichai's *Amen*, Hughes goes so far as to describe Amichai as the "chief character" in a drama of his own composition, drama evidently being at least a convenient metaphor. Hughes in fact tended to see life in terms of drama, in which people had roles, sometimes appearing to be preassigned, and he was drawn to Ancient Greek drama, both in its original form and also as reflected through Roman or later poetic sensibilities, as in Seneca's *Oedipus* or Racine's *Phèdre*.

In an "Apology", written in 1922, Thomas Hardy writes: "let me repeat what I printed more than twenty years ago in a poem entitled 'In Tenebris': If way to the Better there be, it exacts a full look at the Worst..."[1] This also may be held to encapsulate Hughes's philosophy, given his predilection for plays that were concerned with myths associated with catastrophic outcomes. Hughes had been invited to translate Euripides' *Medea*, but had hesitated, losing his chance to do so, which is partly why he responded with alacrity to Jonathan Kent's invitation to work on a version of Racine's *Phèdre*. Queen Phèdre, like Medea, was a woman at the end of her tether, whose revenge was disproportionately terrible, and around whom disastrous happenings unfolded in an apparently inevitable sequence.

Though subscribing to a literalistic approach to translation, Ted Hughes also knew that, unless a play were effective in terms acceptable to a contemporary theatre audience, it could hardly be said to justify its existence. His collaboration with Peter Brook offered scope for experimentation, the most radical example being *Orghast*, where the poet elaborated a language of his own, making possible, he hoped, immediate communication with an audience.[2] Hughes observed that people ordinarily communicated with one another via expressive sounds as much as via meaningful words. Essential messages, often sound-based, although in combination with or linked to recognizable words, depend on tone, emphasis, and so forth. Writers, however, are obliged to employ a given language, even if emotionally intensified by means of phonic devices, including alliteration and assonance, often linked to imagery.

When translating poetry, Hughes was concerned with accessing *the poem itself*, almost as a living creature, nurtured by its own linguistic environment. (He likened this to hunting.) For Hughes, the way forward may have been to adhere to the literal version, but it is clear from his translation of plays that other aspects, more immediately relatable to audience identification with the matter of the play, took precedence. In a copy of the Faber edition of *Phèdre* that he gave me, he had swiftly inscribed changes in the script, made while working with the actors, learning from actors being as important as the source text itself, or as versions by other translators, although he conscientiously also referred to the latter.

Lucius Annaeus Seneca (*c.*4BC–AD65) was a Roman statesman, stoic philosopher and tragic poet, as well as a noted rhetorician. Seneca's speeches have not survived, but much of his verse and prose (treatises and letters) has, as have his tragedies, which were designed for reading or recitation rather than for staged presentation. Most of the plays are drawn from Greek mythology, but Seneca uses an elaborate rhetoric, compensating for the lack of action, alien to the Greek model, which often dwelt on gory details. He was much appreciated as well for his epigrammatic style and use of paradox, and his drama was familiar in the sixteenth century, at a time when Greek tragedy, on the whole, had lost much of its currency. The plays, in their entirety, were translated into English during the Tudor period. T.S. Eliot, who, as is well known, was vitally interested in the possibilities of poetic drama, wrote two important essays on Seneca: "Seneca in Elizabethan Translation" and "Shakespeare and the Stoicism of Seneca".[3] It is probable that Hughes, a great admirer of Eliot, about whom he wrote illuminatingly, studied these.

All eight plays of Seneca that have survived are adapted from the work of other playwrights, *Oedipus* being based on Sophocles' *Oedipus Tyrannus*. Seneca, however, discards, rearranges and, in general, uses the material as he sees fit, his dramatic writings influencing the development of the tragic form in the age of Shakespeare, being notorious for their grotesqueries, scenes of violence and horror, *Oedipus* furnishing several blood-curdling instances of this. Seneca's fascination with magic, death and the supernatural was also often imitated by Elizabethan playwrights.

It was this somewhat unpromising mixture that Peter Brook confronted, and it is not hard to see why Ted Hughes should have accepted the commission to collaborate in the production of *Oedipus*, this project inaugurating a partnership between poet-translator and director, even if the actual circumstances, in this instance, were problematical.

There had been an earlier association between the two. In a memoir, Brook had written:

> *Hughes had been working with us in Paris for several months and was deeply touched by how the seemingly incomprehensible syllables from Ancient Greek with which we were experimenting could carry rich layers of meaning simply through the quality of their sound. The play he then wrote for us to perform at Persepolis,* Orghast, *had fragmentary archetypal situations drawn from ancient myths, but the words were all his own, captured, he would say, in the strata of the brain where deep-rooted semantic forms arise, at the moment when they are becoming coated with shape and sonority but prior to the intervention of the higher levels of the cortex, where concepts emerge.*[4]

This alludes, of course, primarily to their later project, *Orghast*, but also to time spent by Hughes with Brook in Paris, when he attended Brook's experimental studio, the Bouffes du Nord, sketching a series of situations which the actors duly performed. For Brook, Hughes was a fount of invention; for Hughes, Brook's studio was, one imagines, a kind of therapeutic environment, if that be not too dismissive a way of describing it. Brook's comments on "the seemingly incomprehensible syllables from Ancient Greek" reminds one of the desire of many translators to find a means of representing in one's native language –that is, with quite different linguistic tools – what is so vibrant in another language. Hughes's experiments with "Orghast", an invented form of speech, constitute his most concerted attempt to find a solution to an intractable problem, getting actors to respond to sound, rather than conventionally meaningful words.

But whether or not *Orghast* itself, as a kind of culmination of Brook's and Hughes's collaboration, may be regarded as successful, an ability to hear what was going on and to relate it to the action taking place on stage was among Hughes's most valuable assets and is well displayed in his re-adaptation of *Oedipus*, of which Brook writes:

> *It seems the opposite pole from US [an earlier, controversial theatrical production of Brook's] and yet to me the two pieces of theatre are strangely related. There is nothing in common in their idiom, but the subject matter is almost identical: the struggle to avoid facing the truth. Whatever the cost, a man marshals everything at his disposal to skid away from the simple recognition of how things are. What is this extraordinary phenomenon at the very root of our way of existing? Is any other subject so urgent, so vital for us to understand now, today? Is Oedipus' dilemma something to do with the past?*[5]

The political implications, so appealing to Brook, were important to Hughes, too. Both director and translator-playwright saw *Oedipus* in contemporary terms and the earlier version by David Anthony Turner simply did not suit Brook's purpose, which is why he approached Hughes for a new translation.[6]

Ted Hughes has left an extensive account of the negotiation as well as of his experience of working with Brook. His adaptation was first performed by the National Theatre Company in March 1968, with John Gielgud in the title role and Irene Worth as Queen Jocasta. He describes the circumstances:

> *Peter Brook had clear ideas about the type of production he wanted, and when he found the translation [by Turner] did not quite suit them he invited me in to go over and adapt..., and after some tentative false starts, we found the only way forward was for me to go back to the original Seneca, eking out my Latin with a Victorian crib, and so make a completely new translation.*[7]

Brook got the actors to study the play in the "Victorian crib". As Hughes notes further, "I was in complete sympathy with Peter Brook's guiding idea, which was to make a text that would release whatever inner power this story, in its plainest, bluntest form, still has, and to unearth if we could, the ritual possibilities within it." It appears, however, from this document, that Hughes was also embarrassed at a commission that must involve "revising" the work of another translator, inevitably disrupting whatever consistency the latter had managed to establish. Also apparent is Hughes's need for more immediate contact with the source text itself, Seneca's Latin, taking advantage of his own school Latin, a relatively primitive tool. Also worth noting is Brook's determination to rehearse the actors, using the source text as a script, even when (or perhaps because) this was virtually incomprehensible to them. Hughes's remark about the ritual possibilities of the text reminds us that anthropology was his main subject as a student at Cambridge and that his interest in translation, in the first place, may be said to have been triggered by his encounter with the anthropologist Bleek's transcriptions and literalistic renditions of Bushman lore.

Hughes's approach to Seneca's play was "organic", in that the words were for him a clothing for archaic passions, rather than poetry or rhetoric in their own right. His Introduction to the play offers some clues. Hughes notes that the original play,

> Sophocles' Oedipus, *would not have been so suitable for his and Brook's experiment as is Seneca's, the Greek world saturating Sophocles too thoroughly, so that the evolution of his play seems complete... On the other hand, the figures in Seneca's* Oedipus *are Greek only by convention: by nature they are more primitive than aboriginals. They are a spider people scuttling among hot stones. The radiant moral world of Sophocles is simply not present here...* [8]

This comment may not be much to the liking of Classicists, but is a product of Hughes's distinctive vision of the play, drawing on Seneca's own representation of the Greek source. Hughes, somewhat perfunctorily in his Introduction, relates it to historical circumstances. Most important, though, is his last paragraph, in which he indicates that he was remaining as close as possible to the source text, accessed through Miller's literalistic prose translation: "I ran a course widely parallel to the original, touching it here and there, and in a style suited to the way the members of the chorus were deployed all over the theatre. Otherwise the text comes closely out of the original, with much deletion, little addition." As he himself notes, he did add passages to Jocasta's part and in the Choruses, evidently responding as much to Brook's conception of this supposedly obsolete play as to the ensemble energy generated by the company.

It is not so much that his work with Brook is relatable to his interest in translation, as that his interest in translation and theatre relates to a need to go beyond a virtuoso mastery of conventional diction. Apparent, too, is his concern with genre-mixing, translation of remote material into terms apprehensible to a modern audience – Seneca's subject matter is remote – posing special problems of interest to Hughes.

In an interview Hughes refers to Brook's interest in Seneca's *Oedipus*, calling the latter "a very primitive, raw shape of a drama". [9] He describes how he set about producing a stageworthy play, in particular the contribution of the actors and also the contractual obligation to come up with a viable stage presentation of the drama. He refers frankly to his cuts in the source text ("we ended up – finally, with a very short play"), resulting in the creation of a new, essentialist language ("a rigid sort of ugly language"), in the interest of producing a play playable by contemporary actors:

> It was my idea in the translation to do that – to find some way of discarding the ornateness and the stateliness... and to bring out some quite thin but raw presentation of the real core of the play. And in doing that, I shed every mythological reference, which shortened the play by about a third. I shortened every sentence. In fact, I discarded sentence structure. ... I didn't have to imagine a whole new dramatic language... the actors were performing my translation all the time I was translating. So I came up first of all with one version of a part of it, that seemed to me very bare, and to have got through to something essential, and they began to perform and rehearse it, and I began to feel – [we] were driving towards some intense situation in the middle of the play – that this language began to seem too elaborate. And I stripped it again... and this process went on and on and on. I went through many, many drafts until, finally, I was down to about 250 words – that's what it felt like – and a rigid, sort of ugly language, which somehow seemed to come out of this central situation... And [we] ended up, finally, with a very short play, which just was about ... this central situation, this little naked knot. ... So the play finally just had to be performed like an express train.

An impressionistic account maybe, but there is something almost ad-hoc about all this, as there surely had to be if anything at all was to result, the project itself being so complex, bridging a centuries-long gulf and diverse notions of genre.

As noted, Brook got the actors to study and perform the play initially in the literalistic Miller version, one that suited Hughes as a starting point too: "I was now adapting an amalgam of the original, of Miller's version, of Mr. Brook's conception of the play, and my own conception of the play." Brook writes that "[Hughes] was guided by the principle that our own society has more in common with Nero's squalid, murderous Rome than with the radiant moral world of Sophocles's Greece."

In the Tudor period, Seneca's *Oedipus* had been translated by Alexander Neville (1544-1614).[10] Neville, sixteen at the time, states that he translated *Oedipus* to be acted at Cambridge. In his "Preface to the Reader", he lists a number of points, typically made by translators. Whether Hughes read this translation, I do not know, but it seems not unlikely, since he was drawn to the Renaissance. On the other hand, since Neville's version might also have been too far removed from the source text, it seems likely that Hughes's primary source was the Latin itself, in conjunction with Miller's somewhat dated but scholarly prose translation.

The relationship between the Miller and the Hughes may be gleaned from the extract below from Act Two, in which King Oedipus, in dialogue with Creon, Queen Jocasta's brother, calls for expiation for the murder of his predecessor Laius, in the hope that this might bring about deliverance from the scourge afflicting Thebes. Oedipus himself having unwittingly killed his father Laius, afterwards marrying his mother, Jocasta, Laius's widow, although the relationship was unknown to him. The lineation of the published version has been retained, since it was supervised by Hughes. First, Hughes:

OEDIPUS:

> *The movers the guides the lawgivers   are above*
> *they are demanding expiation for this murder*
> *vengeance for Laius   the King of Thebes*
> *where is the man*
>
> *you great gods   you who choose Kings from among*
> *men and set them up and keep them in power*
> *come down and hear these words   you who made*
> *this whole Universe and the laws we have to live and*
> *die in   hear me and you   great burning*
> *watcher who look after the seasons of this earth*
> *who give sap and blood its strength   who pace out*
> *the centuries   and you who govern darkness   and*
> *you   muscle of the earth   who move and speak*
> *in the winds and in water   and you who manage the*
> *dead   be with me now   hear these words I*
> *speak now*
>
> *let no walls hold peace for the man whose hands killed*
> *King Laius   wherever he goes let him be luckless*
> *unprotected   hounded by every evil   let his*
> *genius desert him   let every land reject him   let*

him marry in shame   let his children be born in
shame   let his bed be a torture   a pit and a
rack of shame   and let him deal as bloodily with his
own father   as he dealt with Laius   let him
suffer to the last   wrench everything   and nothing
could be worse than this   everything that I have
escaped   for that man forgiveness no longer exists

by the power of the sea   you who guard my
homeland on every side   by you highest god of the
lightbeams you voice of the oracle   by the
kingdom which I now rule   by the gods of the home
I left   I make an oath   let my father live to
enjoy his old age and his throne in peace   let my
mother never marry any other husband   only as I
dig out this criminal only as I tear the full penalty out
of his living body   only as I avenge Laius

tell it again   where did the murder happen   how
did it happen   open combat   treachery   tell it

Miller:

Now at Heaven's command let the crime be expiated. Whoever of the
gods dost look with favour upon kingdoms – though, thou whose are
the laws of the swift-revolving heavens; and thou, greatest glory of the
unclouded sky, who presidest over the twelve signs in thy changing
course, who dost unroll the slow centuries with swift wheel; and thou,
his sister, ever faring opposite to thy brother, Phoebe, night-wanderer;
thou whom the winds obey, who over the level deep dost speed thy azure
car; and thou who dost allot homes devoid of light – do ye all attend:
Him by whose hand Laius fell may no peaceful dwelling, no friendly
household gods, no hospitable land in exile entertain; over shameful
nuptials may he lament and impious progeny; may he, too, slay his
own father with his own hand and do – can aught heavier be entreated?
– whatever I have fled from. There shall be no place for pardon. I swear
by the sway which I now, a stranger, bear, and by that which I aban-
doned; by my household gods; by thee, O father Neptune, who in double

stream dost play against my shores on either side with scanty waves.
And do thou thyself come as witness to my words, thou who dost inspire
the fate-speaking lips of Cirrha's priestess: So may my father spend
peaceful age and end his days secure on his lofty throne; so may
Merope know the nuptial torches of her Polybus alone, as by no grace
shall the guilty one escape my hand. But tell me, where was the impious
crime committed? Did he die in open battle or by treachery?

Hughes, then, attempted to adjust the Turner version, but in the end found it
"more convenient" to go back to the Latin source text and the prose version of
it by Miller. In the absence, initially, of a satisfactory modern acting version,
Brook used the latter text in rehearsal, Hughes also finding it handy as a basis
for his own version, referring, as best he could, to Seneca's Latin, which, in
the Loeb, is printed en face. Brook, as we have seen, rehearsed the actors at
"full tilt". Like Brook, Hughes saw the play as a manifestation of a universal
myth, in an archaically pure form. In the copy he gave me, he wrote these
grimly joking lines:

Jocasta wails, Oedipus howls
They sound like two horrible fowls...

...

So I say, so I sing,
Like a bird
Who got on quite well
       Without uttering a word.

This offers a clue to his vision of the play as elemental, and to his procedure in
producing a modern version, in a reduced language. Hughes also acknowledges his debt to Peter Brook and his associates: "Without his suggestions,
his judging and cutting, his theatre experience and his conscience, the thing
wouldn't exist..." [11] One sees from this that Brook's judgement may well have
prompted some of Hughes's cuts in the source text. The actors' contributions,
too, receive acknowledgment: "Certain deadlocks in their parts were
brilliantly solved by Irene Worth (Jocasta), Sir John Gielgud (Oedipus), and
Colin Blakely (Creon)." He adds, in a tribute to the ensemble playing
achieved by Brook: "Everybody involved gradually developed a common feeling about the play. ... after a bit of fluid trial and error, the words crystallized
suddenly in a way that has been difficult to alter since." He is surely describing collaborative inspiration, by no means wholly dependent on his own literary skills, but making use of those, as of other factors. The main point,

however, seems to be Hughes's "sympathy with Brook's guiding idea, which was to make a text that would release whatever inner power this story, in its plainest, bluntest form, still has, and to unearth ... the ritual possibilities within it..."

Hughes's brief Introduction to the Faber edition of *Oedipus* offers additional clues. Seneca suited him better than Sophocles, as he points out: "Seneca hardly notices the intricate moral possibilities of his subjects. Nevertheless, while he concentrates on tremendous rhetorical speeches and stoical epigrams, his imagination is quietly producing something else – a series of epic descriptions that contain the raw dream of Oedipus, the basic, poetic, mythical substance of the fable..." Hughes's scholarly interests inform these observations and the mainspring of his translation is revealed, the clarity of a vision in accord with that of Peter Brook, this going some way to explain the power of the translation, noted by reviewers of this play. With regard to *Oedipus*, Hughes himself, as we have seen, concludes that his text "comes loosely out of the original, with much deletion, little addition... I ran a course widely parallel to the original, touching here and there, and in a style suited to the way the members of the chorus were deployed all over the theatre." So, he adapted his script to Brook's production (described in detail, along with descriptions of the various exercises devised by Brook for use in training the actors).

This project is unusually well documented.[12] Lawrence Olivier, Director of the National Theatre, had hoped to direct it, but illness obliged him to appoint a substitute, this being Peter Brook. Since the script was not to Brook's liking, he invited Ted Hughes to revise it. Hughes, for his part, describes the process as a collaborative one, but the invitation from Tynan clearly came at a good moment. As Hughes notes, "[Brook] remembered my old ideas about the Greek tragedies – simplified & done full tilt..." By "full tilt", Hughes did not mean carelessly, or in a spirit of abandon; on the contrary, what he had in mind was *total* concentration, putting one in mind of his advice to young poets or teachers of poetry that students be challenged to write at top speed: "The chief aim should be to develop the habit of all-out, flowing exertion, or a short, concentrated period, in a definite direction." Hughes describes his first meeting with Brook and his co-director, Geoffrey Reeves. The narrative presents his negative reaction to Turner's version of the play with, at the same time, his appreciation of it as "abrupt, compressed, [having] a kind of artificiality that was quite powerful & lively, almost a stylishness at times..." That he was able to proceed was surely due to his ability sharply to sense the dynamism of the source text through another painstaking version. He remarks that Brook, "like me, had been attracted by the explosive exclamatory expressionistic moments in the Turner". He adds: "I wasn't able to provide as much of the abrupt explosiveness at that early moment he was dreaming of... But it was the single stylistic principle that dictated how I finally wrote." Even a cursory examination of the script confirms this. Hughes may be said to have invented a language, as he did far more radically, in "Orghast". But the language he used in translating Seneca's text is, perhaps, more closely related to that which he also developed later in co-translating work by the Hungarian poet János Pilinzsky, where he had a source-language collaborator and where he knew the poet personally and so could proceed with confidence. The reduced language adopted by Hughes markedly contrasts with Shakespeare's which is unprecedentedly copious, Hughes being drawn both to copiousness and economy of diction.

He describes how he began to work on Turner's script: "All I seemed to be doing at that stage was making it poetically pretty & literary". It is interesting that Hughes, somewhat against the grain, had allowed himself to be drawn into what seemed to be a thankless task; one assumes that this was due to certain priorities having been established earlier, an interest in Seneca, perhaps encouraged by Eliot's essays. We do, however, have Hughes's candid discussion and the process whereby he was drawn in: "In the desperate labour of comparison & rising to the occasion & self-transformation, I tunnelled further in a week or two than I had tunnelled in all my previous play writing. It was precisely what I needed. ... I began to feel, here & there, confidence. Just the odd sentence." Despite his tentativeness, he continued to revise the Turner text. Brook, however, mentioned that he "thought the dialogue lumbering & wooden & horribly wordy". In a conciliatory spirit, Hughes "set to pushing & pulling at bits ... just chopping and teasing it here and there now & again..." Finally, he came up with a draft, at which point Brook "told how he'd been taking the actors through the Latin & the Miller version, word for word, and spoken what a revelation it was. Drop the Turner." Inexorably, Hughes, though his knowledge of the Classical languages was rudimentary, was being driven back to the source or to the version of it by Miller. This seems to have puzzled many commentators, but Hughes was of course trying to compensate for his scholarly deficiencies by "reading around" the text, and by consulting others. He was especially drawn to literal interpretations by scholars with few literary pretensions but with a concern for semantic and even syntactic exactitude, Miller's text fitting the bill.

Hughes later read his new version of the play to Brook, Gielgud, Worth, Turner and others involved in the production. This reading by the translator was edifying, but it is Hughes's own self-deprecatory description that is particularly revealing, as well as his remarks regarding Brook's shock tactics. Brook "described my monotonous carry on as a 'true reading' – setting it comparatively against Sir J's reading of the opening, & much else – which was simply stylish reading. Brook already upsetting Sir J's confidence in his lifelong developed verse-voice; one can hardly imagine an actor less well suited to Brook's approach to acting than Gielgud." Hughes describes this revered performer's dilemma movingly: "He felt & said quite openly that he'd never be able to do it. He needed such guidance, he needed so much support and leading by the hand – he made a joke of what a perfect child he was, how he needed to be told & reassured at every point."

The problem was similar with the anglicized American actress Irene Worth, as Queen Jocasta. Despite the simplicity and directness of her acting, "she seemed to me made of rep. mannerisms, West End society theatre & theatre society. I didn't see how she could manage Jocasta... primitive, harsh; Irene seemed a vivacious society doll..." Hughes vividly describes a particular rehearsal session:

> Brook mentioned the method of having all actors simply jabber their lines until they had got thoroughly absorbed by the play, deeply understood it – only then beginning to bring the right expression into their speech. He spoke with despair about the actors – of the problem of getting them to drop their bag of tricks, – of the near impossibility of this... the idea of getting actors to speak rawly, nakedly. His real gift as a director is to direct his actors' minds towards a certain end, so all their work becomes natural. He directed our minds towards the ideas of fate, destiny, the strange tangle about the womb, the Vietnam terror of the plague, the religious overtones in particular of many epithets. He pushed towards the largest deepest atmosphere of the play, so we ploughed through it all day. [13]

Noteworthy, I think, at this point, is the emphasis on rapidly traversing the play ("having all actors simply jabber their lines"). Brook evidently was determined to get the actors to feel their way into the text at a deeper level, having first familiarized themselves, as it were, with its contours. Hughes alludes to Lorca's essay on "*duende*" especially in connection with the version of the latter's poetic drama, *Blood Wedding*, directed by Tim Supple. In this lecture, Lorca attempts to describe this quality:

The duende... *is a power, not a work; it is a struggle, not a thought. I have heard an old maestro of the guitar say, 'The duende is not in the throat, the duende climbs up inside you, from the soles... [I]t is not a question of ability, but of true, living style, of blood, of the most ancient culture of spontaneous creation.*[14]

In the light of the dictionary definition of *duende*, "a ghost, an evil spirit, inspiration, magic, fire" seems hardly adequate!

It may be difficult to grasp the validity of Hughes's comment on the Greek playwright, perhaps because the myth itself is so troubling that one is impelled to read swiftly, even hastily, rather than lingeringly. What Hughes may have had in mind was also, in part, a desire to convey Brook's directorial sense of Seneca's more elemental version of the myth. One is struck by Hughes's characterization of Seneca's figures as "a spider people, scuttling among hot stones", and his sense of Seneca's play as containing "the *raw* dream of Oedipus". Whatever else may be true, it is evident that the Roman author's text stimulated Hughes's poetic imagination as the Greek source failed to do.

The Hughes and Turner versions look alike, both transcribed in highly punctuated prose, suggestive of a similar basic strategy. However, Hughes's was more distinctly articulated, spaces frequently indicated between the clusters of words, whereas Turner's runs on without breaks, if with a plethora of dashes. Brook's rapid-delivery method supplied the means of bypassing or overcoming the educated response of professionally trained actors and stimulated or provoked reactions at a more instinctual level; in his *The Shifting Point* (London, 1987), Brook had referred to an intervention by Gielgud, noting that "the words had flown out of John's mouth before he could stop them [...] In John, tongue and mind work so closely together that it is sufficient for him to think of something for it to be said. Everything in him is moving all the time, at lightning speed – a stream of consciousness flows from him without pause. His flickering, darting tongue reflects everything around and inside him... [H]is tongue is the sensitive instrument that captures the most delicate shade of feeling in his acting..."

Naturalness of this order is achievable not only by disrupting conventions but also by rigorous training, the ingenious exercises devised by Brook also directed towards achieving this end. The approach also appealed to Hughes who was aware of the many obstacles in the path of accessing deeper levels of the self and was attracted by disciplines that assisted him in overcoming this. Gielgud, too, was convinced, judging from Brook's testimony:

"[His reaction] was immediate. He plunged in. He tried, he tried humbly, clumsily, with all he could bring. He was no longer the star, a superior being. He was quite simply there, struggling with his body, as the others would be later with their words, with an intensity and a sincerity that were his own..."

Though Hughes, as we have seen, expressed appreciation of the Turner version, he felt obliged to return to the source, or at least to Miller's early prose account of it, which Brook, in the interim period, in rehearsal, had used as a provisional rehearsal script. Here, as an example, is the opening of the play, setting the scene in a devastated Thebes. Oedipus is speaking.

Miller:

> *Now night is driven away; the hesitant sun returns, and rises, sadly veiling his beams in murky clouds; with woeful flame he brings a light of gloom and will look forth upon our homes stricken with ravenous plague, and day will reveal the havoc which night has wrought.*

Hughes puts this speech in the mouth of the Chorus, visualizing the situation of Thebes and trying to represent it more immediately than Miller, whose concern must have been to produce an acceptable ad-verbum English version of the Latin. Turner omits it, beginning his play at a later point. (Omission is also resorted to by Hughes, but not in this instance.)

Hughes:

> *Night is finished   but day is reluctant   the sun drags itself up out of that filthy cloud   it stares down at our sick earth   it brings a gloom not light*
> *beneath it our streets homes temples gutted with the plague   it is one huge plague pit   the new heaps of dead spewed up everywhere   hardening in the sickly daylight*

Hughes proceeds swiftly to the confrontation with Jocasta, who chides Oedipus for his faintheartedness. His script suggests a kind of musical score:

> JOCASTA: *Oedipus   you are the man we rely on   you are the King, the strength   if we have strength*
>
> *The heavier the threat the stronger we should find you to bear the threat for every challenge an answer   a King cannot sit wringing his hands reproaching the gods   weeping like a baby   wanting to die*

Turner:

> JOCASTA: *Oedipus, my husband. What use is complaining? It only makes bad things worse. To my mind the essence of being a king is to take on challenges. The more your throne tremble, the faster your power and majesty slip into decline, then all the more fearlessly should you take your stand, controlled, unwavering. Running away is no behaviour for a man.*

Miller:

> JOCASTA: *What boots it, husband, to make woe heavier by lamentation? This very thing, methinks, is regal – to face adversity and, the more dubious thy station and the more the greatness of empire totters to its fall, the more firm to stand, brave with unfaltering foot. 'Tis no manly thing to turn the back to Fortune.*

Both Miller and Turner have translated the prose sense of the passage, but Hughes's version conveys both the sense and forcefulness of Jocasta's urging, constituting also a taunt and challenge that recall her son-husband Oedipus to his duty as a king and his pride as a man. Hughes eliminates cliché, not always avoided by Turner, partly through lexical economy, deleting inessentials and visualizing the situation in mythical rather than domestic terms. He has updated Miller's language, which is replete with what Ezra Pound called "King James fustian" (for example, "What boots it"). In short, Hughes seeks to invest surface meaning with emotional reality that will appeal to a modern audience, in a language accessible to it.

X

Orghast
The Search for a Universal Language

Performed by an international cast of actors, directed by Peter Brook, *Orghast* was the first major public project of the latter's Paris-based International Centre for Theatre Research (CRIT). The play is about the Titan Prometheus, who stole fire from Zeus and gave it to mortals for their use. This myth has been treated by a number of ancient sources, in which Prometheus is credited with (or blamed for) playing a pivotal role in the early history of humankind, and it was scheduled for performance at the ruined palace of Darius the Great in Persepolis during Iran's Shiraz/Persepolis festival, after having been evolved by the company in rehearsal in Paris. The play draws on *Prometheus Bound*, the first part in a lost trilogy by Aeschylus, and is written in a language invented by Ted Hughes for the purpose and based on Avesta, an ancient Iranian language, the language in which the Zoroastrian Holy Scriptures are written.

What concerned Hughes, or caught his imagination, was the opportunity or challenge to reinvent, as it were, what Walter Benjamin, in his landmark essay, "The Task of the Translator", called an *Ursprache*.[1] Hughes had called it a "universal language of understanding" in his Introduction to the programme of the Poetry International readings in London in 1967. he returned to the theme later, when, as Poet Laureate, officially representative of the Crown, he addressed the Asian Poetry Festival in Bangladesh. Attempting to put the interest in foreign poetry into a historical context, he talked of the need to "find in poetry a single common language of fellow feeling... of shared essential humanity". For Hughes, translation, rather than being an instrument of colonialization, as post-colonial critics have sometimes depicted it (at least as regards translation into the former dominant imperial language, English), was one of understanding and cross-fertilization in a period following two catastrophically destructive wars.

It is this faith or hope that underlies Hughes's interest also in discovering common linguistic roots, a means of communication or a language capable of enunciating meaning and making an impact. A similar search appeared to be underway in the theatre. Both Brook and Hughes were interested in the experiments, for instance, of the French theatrical innovator Antonin Artaud, who envisaged theatre as a total work of art, a uniting of all arts, flooding the spectator's senses in a state of "total immediacy, a wholly auditory language". Also to be taken into account was the work of the contemporary Polish director Jerzy Grotowski, whose views on acting, as relayed by Brook, appealed greatly to Hughes, with Grotowski's determination to tap something deeper than specific cultural responses, to eschew reliance on technological wizardry and return to the expressive potential of the human being, with only his or her voice and body as instruments.[2] And of course Classical Greek theatre appealed, with its use of dance and mime, as well as the poetry of language.

Ted Hughes was thus broadly in sympathy with Brook's objectives, and their collaboration, in Seneca's *Oedipus* and then in *Orghast,* were the key moments in the search for directness of expressive means. Even though he was drawn to the amplitude of Shakespearean diction, it cannot be said that Hughes ever forgot the linguistic experiment undertaken with Brook. In fact, he rewrote the text in a language described by A.C.H. Smith as "spare, asyntactic and not always comprehensible", full of "semantic ambiguities" and "foregrounding the sounds of the words – a style calling to mind Joyce's 'stream of consciousness'".[3] Hughes's theatrical experience left its mark on his own work as a poet, most obviously in the cycle of poems, directly related to *Orghast*, "Prometheus on his Crag", where "The text moves forward by virtue of consonantal shifts, or even by straightforward repetition." According to Paul Bentley: "This partial breakdown in structure constitutes a first step towards the outer limits of the norms of linguistic communication."[4] Bentley notes further: "The invented language was based on instinctual sounds; what Hughes was aiming for here was a purely 'semiotic' language, a language of 'vocal or kinetic rhythm', stripped of its figurative or conceptual function."

"Orghast", however, was a big advance even on this. Hughes remarked: "English was hopeless. It could never have come near it... The first vocabulary of *Orghast* was a language purged of the haphazard associations of English, which continually tries to supplant experience and truth with the mechanisms of its own autonomous life."[5] There seems to be a connection with the "super-ugly" style of *Crow*, with "Hughes attempting to rediscover an ancient animal language, which would not become fixed in set phrases when arranged syntactically", the aim being "to evoke the truth and reality of experience". So, abandoning conventional English, he embarked on a voyage of discovery, which he here and there attempts to describe. For instance, in an interview with Tom Stoppard, he noted that "the best words are words you invent immediately, your mind fixed on the thing or state you want to express", that is, in a state of absent concentration.[6] He wondered about this, but clearly took it that he was at least on the right track. "Orghast is an *ursprache*, an elemental, original language capable of communicating, empathically, meanings, or at least certain 'basic mental states'."

Even if there was no obvious sequel to this work, there can be no doubting the seriousness of Hughes's involvement with such experimentation at this point in his career. He imported into it much of what he had earlier learnt in translating Pilinszky's poetry, including what the poet himself had said about having acquired his Hungarian from a brain-damaged relative. Peter Brook had had a somewhat similar experience, when he received the writings of an autistic woman. I have not seen these texts, but as a translator have myself quite frequently been vouchsafed a fresh view of my own language, via a translation into it, before I have resisted the urge to domesticate or revise the text into acceptable English, a procedure likely to produce a sense of dissatisfaction, as though an essential otherness has been sacrificed in the interest of enhanced intelligibility.

Orghast, a play in a language of the same name, near to one of pure sound, based on the myth of Prometheus, centres on a tale of repression and rebirth which parallels, continues and inverts the victory of the male over the female principle, as told in Hesiod's *Theogony*. The play, as noted, was scripted for a performance at the Shiraz Festival in Persepolis, near Teheran, directed by Peter Brook, in Summer 1971. Ted Hughes joined Brook in Iran for the festival. An important source of the play, as also noted, was Aeschylus's *Prometheus Bound*, and it was retold by Hughes in an invented language, the story enacted in the body of the Titan, chained to a rock.

Orghast may be said to have evolved in part from *The Conference of the Birds*, a Persian Sufi story, which had been a repertory piece for Brook's international group of actors in Paris.[7] This could be performed impromptu, as an exercise or to entertain visitors, with no words to remember, only a scenario and sounds. Whether *The Conference of the Birds* was already in the repertory before Ted Hughes's involvement is uncertain, but in any case, he came up with sounds for it, possibly ur-*Orghast*. This suggests that the direction, or one of the directions, in which Brook was going, coincided with certain interests of Hughes, which related to translation and his notion of literalism or quasi-identity with sources. Translation involved a "search for the truth", recalling also the shamanistic search, since it involves the notion of a journey and a return with authentic gains.

With *Orghast*, apparently, Hughes was trying to move beyond absorbing masterworks, such as *Sir Gawain and the Green Knight*. He did not tackle the *Mahabharata*, in spite of Brook's urgings that he do so, nor did he take more than the first steps towards a version or adaptation of *Gilgamesh*, but he had his eye on them all. In 1994, Brook, as mentioned, sent Hughes some poems by a "45 year old autistic lady, who had virtually no communication with others, minimal IQ, cerebral palsy…" In the same letter, Brook comments: "It all comes out of 'The Man Who'", this being his adaptation of the neurological anecdote told by Oliver Sacks in his 1985 book, *The Man Who Mistook His Wife for a Hat*, an adaptation regarded by Hughes as Brook's masterpiece. Both Brook and Hughes wondered where the words came from, if the writer had no verbal exchange with the world, with its suggestion that there was an accessible centre, intrinsic to human beings, where communicable sounds were generated. In the interview with Stoppard, Hughes commented:

I was interested in the possibilities of a language of tones and sounds, without specific conceptual or perceptual meaning, long before, but for drama not for poetry. In poetry this sort of experiment remains meaningless, for such a language needs a body of precise but unexpressed meaning behind it – such as is supplied by religious intention (as in mantras, etc.) or by action.

Drama, that is, is not just a matter of an author's words but of the combined effect of acting, directing, and the text.

As regards his dissatisfaction with English, Hughes noted:

The idea was to build up a small range of sound which we could then organise rhythmically. We started with a fairly complicated narrative, using several myths which we blended together into one cosmology. The Prometheus myth was one, and also the mythology or cosmology of Manichaean writings. Brook wanted to open up in actors the stores of meaningful expression and feeling which ordinary language just skates over. They worked for a long time with a dozen or so set syllables that had no fixed meaning and therefore infinitely variable potential meaning.

Hughes detailed how he had chanced on words and constructed others. "The good words", he had observed, "are those you invent immediately – blind –

your mind completely fixed on the thing or state you want to express. Out of these root words, you compound others. Some of these are good, others not so good. Afterwards, the words I invented blind turned out to be compounds of the first roots I established." This experience seemed to confirm what he had instinctively accessed, that the knowledge is intrinsic, but that access to it necessitates an almost mediumistic state of mind.

The relevance of all this to translation may not be immediately apparent, except that Hughes touches specifically on this very issue: "In literature you hear it all, but translated, as though literature were a more formal ordering and translation of what you hear otherwise. But in literature, you don't hear it just as language; you hear it as a system of attitudes and feeling and ideas and so on. Whereas in ordinary speech you hear it as a purely musical, animal chord, to which you respond immediately – but you understand in a very complicated way...." It seems as if he were translating back from translations to what underlies them.

If *Orghast*, in its esotericism, can hardly be claimed to have solved the problems of preserving the colloquial expressiveness of ordinary speech, it at least suggests a line of approach. No excerpt can give more than an impression of a text that was part of a total spectacle, as performed at the Shiraz Festival, for a detailed account of which the reader is directed to A.C.H. Smith's account.[8] Avesta cannot be transcribed, but a simulacrum is provided, "an invocation to the fecund earth and pregnant women", annotated as Irene Worth pronounced it. It moves very slowly:

IMÂM IMÂM IMÂM Immaawwmmm – full cheek, letting the sound go up
the nose and round the forehead, as though in a cave
AAT ZAM aat-at zaawmmmm
GENABIS HAHRA YAZAMAIDE gennaawbish
YA NAW BARAITÍ YAWSCHA naaooow; yaaaowstcha, the last syllable
snapped upward in tone, above the tonic note of incantation, and glot-
tally stopped
TOI GENAW AHURA MAZDAW taawi; a-hhura
ASHA HA CHA VAIRYAW AW taawi; a-hhura
ASHAT HACHA VAIRYAW TAW vaireeow; taaoooow

XI

The Last Translation
Pushkin's *The Prophet*

Does the shamanic notion of death and resurrection, explored by Hughes in so many contexts and directly addressed in his work on the Bardo, apply also to the notion of translation? Certainly the notion itself was a major concern throughout his life, in his own writing, and in translational explorations, from his early work at Yaddo to what may have been his very last poem, a translation of Pushkin's late visionary poem, "The Prophet".

Translators tend not to view their efforts in such grandiose terms, but the deconstruction of the poem and its reconstruction as a function of the search for equivalences in the target language, is perhaps reminiscent of the shamanic journey. The question is where to go in attempting to reconstitute the source poem, and what is being reconstituted, that is to say, what *is* the source poem? Naturally, the process is not so cut-and-dried; even less, is it two-stage. Hughes tried, almost by force of imagination, to achieve identity between ad-verbum version and source-text. Nevertheless, as is obvious – even when he had convinced himself that he was being quite literal – he inevitably imprinted the version that went out under his name with his personality and style, and even, perhaps, with a suggestion of his preoccupations. It seems fair to say, however, that he also remained close to the vision of those poets whose work he translated, seeking to represent its physical dimensions as well as semantic content. He was able to do so, insofar as what he chose to translate was consistent with his own poetic concerns and development, even if now and then he experimented with work that seemed remote.

Translation, for Hughes, was influenced by his readings in Shamanism, behind which, he suspected, lay Sufism; he wrote: "one might almost say that Shamanism was a barbarized, stray descendant of Sufism", and, in one of the notes to Idries Shah's introduction to his anthology *The Way of the Sufi*, Shah himself observes: "A penetrating perception of the fact that many Sufi ideas have filtered into primitive communities was written by the well-known poet Ted Hughes two years ago."[1] Hughes's interest in Islamic mysticism is attested, among others things, by his work with Peter Brook on Attar's *The Conference of the Birds*, for which Hughes "invented" a bird language – acquisition of the language of animals, especially birds, also being a feature of shamanic training.

While he was drawn to and investigated Sufism, Hughes was more engaged with Shamanism; his early and later interest in *The Tibetan Book of the Dead* surely having more to do with its shamanic than its Buddhist connections. Hughes was particularly interested in the practical use of ecstatic states in self-management and dealing with crises.

As regards literalism, it would seem that Hughes did not engage in the polemics that have preoccupied translators, nor contribute to the debate regarding domestication and foreignization, domestication seen as a colonialistic enterprise which strives to makes familiar and palatable what in reality is alien. It is more, surely, that Hughes believed the essence, the irreducible minimum or wisdom in alien or remote texts, might be conveyed through scrupulous attention to the means of expression. In this connection, he agreed with Nabokov, though he did not put it so polemically. He was not, however, content to limit himself in this way, aware of the larger dimension into which his work fitted, his personal contribution as a poet, and he explored this, altering and expanding it by means of his investigations, translation being an important means of exploration and the translations he produced functioning as notations.

In the case of Hughes's translation of Pushkin's "The Prophet" (*Prorok*), he was provided by myself and Valentina Polukhina with a literal version of the Russian source text and a guide to the pattern of sound and prosody. He remarked that he sensed something "primitive" in Pushkin's sophisticated poetry or in the language, insofar as this could be gleaned from the English versions he had read and the crib with which he was supplied. The indication, I believe, is that he had found a starting point, as with Pilinszky and Amichai, rather than this being a judgment on the nature of Pushkin's mature poetry.

What follows is the conclusion of the Pushkin poem in the ad-verbum version we supplied:

I lay like a corpse in the desert/wilderness,
And the voice of God called out to me/summoned me:
'Arise, prophet, and see, and hear,
Carry out my will,
And passing by sea and land,
Burn the hearts of people with the word.'

Hughes:

> *I lay on stones like a corpse.*
> *There God's voice came to me:*
> *'Stand, Prophet, you are my will.*
> *Be my witness. Go*
> *Through all seas and lands. With the Word*
> *Burn the hearts of the people.'*

Hughes produced three drafts of the translation. To gain some perspective I have compared the final Hughes version closely with versions by other translators, including Dmitry Obolensky, D.M. Thomas, Anthony Briggs, and Alan Myers. Below is an analysis of these six lines, which I am able to supply, having been privy to the translation process. The analysis of this poem is given here as an example of Hughes's approach to foreign texts, indicating the "liberties" he was inclined to take, while remaining loyal to the literal draft with which he was supplied; the tension set up by these two poles was not one he sought to avoid.

Valentina Polukhina and I supplied an additional paragraph of explanation, as follows:

> *Here is rough English for 'The Prophet'. Pushkin wrote it in 1826, at the*
> *time of the Decembrist Rising. The language is quite archaic, Biblical*
> *(Isaiah 6, etc.), unusual for Pushkin, since he is known for bringing*
> *colloquial Russian into the poetry. Legend has it that this poem was in*
> *Pushkin's pocket during a secret interview with the Tsar himself, soon*
> *after the Rising. Pushkin sympathised with the Decembrists, aristo-*
> *cratic reformers, who were also his friends.*

Hughes did not avail himself of our offer to investigate other translations and one cannot be certain as to what extent he used the crib. Possibly, the literal and literate translations were all he needed, but presumably he also made his way through the transliteration of the Cyrillic source text we sent him.

Commentary on the last six lines of Hughes's version:

l.25 *I lay on stones like a corpse.*

Literate:

> *I lay like a corpse in the desert/wilderness,*

Hughes's translation of "desert" or "wilderness" as "stones" is a graphic simplification. He sacrifices, that is, the association of Old Testament prophet and of a desert or wilderness for the sake of a more immediate presentation of the wilderness scene, such as in a painting by, say, El Greco. Again the tactile seems to be at issue. Stones can be felt, except of course that a corpse does not *feel* anything. So the deadness to feeling of the corpse-like self is emphasized. (Myers has: "As corpse-like on the sand I lay.") "Stones" seems to relate more to "wilderness" than to "desert"; Jerusalem's stony, hilly environs perhaps. The line is hard in every sense, and leads directly into the next, though Hughes's version, unlike the original, ends with a full stop.

l.26:

There God's voice came to me

literate:

And the voice of God called out to me / summoned me:

In English, "There" links the two more dramatically than "And". With "There", Hughes modernizes, articulating the drama clearly, with a slight pause at this point, further emphasizing God's final pronouncement. Interestingly, he separates God's voice from the lying on stones or in a wilderness.

Obolensky, too, has a full stop at the end of line 25, but begins line 26 with "And":

And the voice of God called out to me /

Briggs has these two lines as a separate stanza.

With "came to me", Hughes suggests the passivity of the subject, the focus remaining on him, rather than on his turning to God. In spite of the break, there is a greater psychological continuity between these two lines in the Hughes version even than in the original. "Came to me" is suggestive of revelation, yet at the same time is somewhat casual. It came (or occurred) to me is normal enough. But "The voice [personified] came to me" seems slightly unidiomatic. I wonder, therefore, whether Hughes, with his literalistic preferences, was having difficulties with its being the voice of God rather than God himself who called out to me. There is redundancy in the notion of a voice rather than an individual calling. "God's voice came to me" is obviously more logical. But we are here immersed in Biblical language, which often makes a virtue of redundancy.

Both Thomas and Briggs normalize:

And God called out to me [...]; I [...] hearkened to the voice of God.

Hughes's version alone keeps the focus on God's voice.

ll.27-30

Stand, Prophet, you are my will.
Be my witness. Go

> *Through all seas and lands. With the Word*
> *Burn the hearts of the people.'*

Literal:

> *Arise prophet, and see [archaic], and hear,*
> *Fill with will mine [carry out my will]*
> *And passing/wandering by seas and lands*
> *With the word burn the hearts of the people.*

Hughes stays closer to the literal than to the literate: e.g., literate "passing by sea and land" (singular, "Burn the hearts of people with the word"). In the second case, he retains the exact wording but breaks the line, thus highlighting "Word" by placing it at the end, in the penultimate line, this being the only instance where he keeps to the exact wording of the literal/literate, although in one or two other places he merely normalizes the syntax of the literal version.

The lineation and punctuation are dramatic, as in an acting or speaking text. These four lines, in the Pushkin source, run smoothly, metrically regular, without break; Hughes, though, breaks three times, and has two enjambments. "Go", like "Word", is strongly stressed. God's utterance is divided into four declamatory sentences. These are more distinctly articulated in the Hughes version than in Pushkin. Going "through all seas and lands" receives almost as much emphasis as bringing "the Word".

There is, however, an abruptness, even jerkiness, in Hughes's ending, as against the smoothness of the source text, with its Biblical resonances. The Biblical note is audible in Hughes, too, but there is also something makeshift, almost inconclusive, companioning the emphasis and finality, so that one is tempted to ask whether he is not, after all, making the poem his own.

"You are my will" is invention, although the literal's "Fill with my will" or, more accurately, in Obolensky's translation, "be filled with my will", is perhaps rebarbative enough to have precipitated so drastic a solution. "Fill" (or even "be filled") chimes too strongly with "Will". Hughes's formulation, in its abruptness too, echoes some of his characterizations of God or of Crow, in *Crow*, although the context here would not admit the ribald, or carnival grotesqueries of Crow. "Be my witness", a separate sentence, was surely prompted by the "see" and "hear" of the line above. (The use of "see", though, is problematical, because of "seas" in the penultimate line.) So, while making this more explicit, contemporary, at the same time as retaining the Biblical allusiveness, Hughes reverses the order of these two items: "You are my will. / Be my witness," rather than: "Be my witness" (see, and hear) "You are my will

[Be filled with my will]". He is thus able to end two lines with stressed mono-syllabic words, "will" and "Go". "With the Word", helped by the capitalization, constitutes the climax of the poem, the very last line, rhythmically, functioning as a kind of coda. In general the lineation here makes the reader linger, God having set the Prophet in motion.

Interestingly, Hughes has drawn not just on the literate but also on the literal versions with which he was provided. Valentina Polukhina and I were following a method developed by the late Max Hayward when working with the American poet Stanley Kunitz on the translation of Anna Akhmatova's poetry. Hayward had provided Kunitz with literal versions and what he called "literate", or syntactically normalized English versions, of the poems. He also provided Kunitz with cultural and linguistic contextual information and, of course, was available to work with him personally. Hughes did not ask for further assistance, though it seems to me he paid attention to our attempt at a literal account of the poem as he did when working with Yehuda Amichai on the latter's own English versions, or as with János Csokits's literalistic versions of Pilinszky's poems. His own solutions often draw from these cribs rather than from previous attempts to solve the problems, more likely to be embodied in so-called literate versions.

XII
Conclusion

The founding of *Modern Poetry in Translation* was a bold and probably tactically ill-advised initiative, since there was a danger of Hughes being cast at a vulnerable early stage in his career, as someone who gave too much time to what was regarded as a dubious enterprise. If the same was true of Pope or Dryden, there seems to have been no inhibition in their age against functioning also as a translator of poetry. In our time, however, translation is frequently seen as a non- or only semi-creative enterprise, or seen as derivative, though arguably so is all literature. Nevertheless, it may explain why so many writers who also translate do not advertise the fact, investing this slightly disreputable side of their work with an aura of creativity, which is most readily done by aligning translation with their own original work.

Ted Hughes's single "colonizing" effort, if it may be so called, was his re-translation of Juhász's poem, "The Boy Changed into a Stag", working from a pre-existing version rather than directly from the source text itself, to which he had no linguistic access, having no familiarity with Hungarian. In general, Hughes's aim when translating work by other poets was to stay as close as he could to the wording and syntax of the source, a "literalistic" crib being what he required, as a preliminary, from his collaborators. Though Hughes's one might say un-modish approach to the task of translation was unlikely to gain many accolades, he persevered, and it was the absence of publications on the lookout for such scholarly (even pedantic) versions that persuaded him to advocate the establishment of *Modern Poetry in Translation*, and also of the annual Poetry International readings, both of which ventures he hoped would boost the production of "literalistic" ad-verbum versions. Since the source-language poets would also be present at Poetry International to read their work in the source language, what was required were reliably close guides to the sense, as had also been available at the Spoleto Festival. Hughes was keen that *MPT* should be available at the international reading, with a special programme issue, filled with translations of the kind he favoured.

This would provide the audience with primary material relating to what they were hearing and would function also as an aide-memoire, but certainly not as a substitute for the source text, as read by the poets themselves.

Ever the optimist, Hughes believed that what was so clear to him would also be clear to others. His own ambition was to gain access, via translation, to the poetic sensibility of other poets, functioning in other linguistic environments. He believed this sensibility was transferable; at any rate, he saw little to be gained from being offered what were, in fact, interpretations or readings of a foreign poet's works by native poets collaborating with language informants. On a different occasion (for example, with Robert Lowell's *Imitations*) he did acknowledge that these "re-workings" might be of value or interest; but in general he believed the poem itself to be accessible only via "rawly-made", ad-verbum translation. Of course, Hughes acknowledged that some adjustments might be necessary, naturalizing the translations, and since others could not be expected to perform this apparently menial task, he engaged in it himself.

Pope and Dryden have been mentioned, but Hughes's approach was arguably somewhat antithetical to theirs. "A pretty poem Mr Pope, but you must not call it Homer," remarked an English critic of Pope's grandiose translation of the Homeric epic. Today, one imagines, it would not have been so hard for Pope to garner acclaim for this eccentrically scholarly rendering of Homer's verse, even if a few voices of dissent might still rise from the ranks of specialists eager to demonstrate their erudition and stubbornly loyal to the specificities of the source.

The problem is a perennial one: how to transfer a poem from one language to another without so catastrophic a loss that the whole enterprise becomes problematical, since, as Robert Frost famously quipped: "Poetry is what gets lost in translation." So intimately is poetry bound up with the language in which it is written that to aspire to translate a different language seems as foolish as, in another context, it was once considered blasphemous to translate into contemporary vernacular God's Word, originally conveyed in a holy language, Hebrew.

Hughes could not but have been aware of these considerations. As George Steiner shows, the argument against the translation of poetry is an argument against literary translation as such.[1] Even so, there is surely a qualitative difference between translation of prose texts and that of poetry. Various approaches have been favoured regarding the daunting task facing the poetry-translator, a somewhat last-ditch one being that adopted by the

American writer and scholar Stanley Burnshaw.[2] The principal aim, as Burnshaw shows, is to conduct the reader back to "the poem itself, the source text, on the assumption that, with a contextualizing apparatus, this is the best to be hoped for unless a kind of fraud is to be perpetrated on the reader, substituting a critical reading for the authenticity of a source text." Nabokov, in his masterly rendering of Pushkin's novel-in-verse *Eugene Onegin*, although more elaborately, says something similar.[3] As he puts it in his Introduction:

> *I have sacrificed to completeness of meaning every formal element, including the iambic rhythm, whenever its retention hindered fidelity. To my ideal translation I sacrificed everything (elegance, euphony, clarity, good taste, modern usage, and even grammar) that the dainty mimic prizes higher than truth.*

Hughes agreed with this ambition, yet also approved *Imitations*, Lowell's anthology of his own free translations, in which he reconstituted the foreign poems in terms that satisfy the poet, Robert Lowell. Hughes felt that this project, though brilliantly accomplished, did not represent what he really wanted or hoped for, what translation most usefully, in his view, might achieve. One must conclude that both literal and re-creative forms of translation have a place. Nevertheless, it is, at least, interesting that so sophisticated a poet as Hughes should have chosen to differentiate himself from Robert Lowell, whom he admired, and should have devoted so much time (some of it even towards the end of his life, when he knew that little time remained) to making translations which were attacked as reeking of the original and were likely to bring him little credit as an independent artist. One might even claim that translation enabled Hughes to scan territories of the literary imagination otherwise inaccessible even to his panoptic vision.

But this is not a topic on which agreement is likely to be reached. Hughes, who frequently insisted he was getting a lot from translation, followed the original verbally and lineally. This painstaking procedure so little accords with the popular view of the author as a kind of king-player (Hughes being clearly one) that it is not always taken at face value, though Hughes tried hard to show that his ambitions as a translator were limited. It seems that for him translation of poetry was not merely a tribute paid to predecessors or contemporaries, but also a mental discipline. He was interested in methods of disciplining the mind, and translation was one such, in the control of self-expression. Translation, for instance, of the poetry of János Pilinzsky was seen by Hughes as an act that aligned him with the original author's piety. Defending his approach to translating Pilinszky's poetry, Hughes admitted its radicalism, but insisted: "[I]t was a natural decision, I think, in translating a poet whose chief characteristics are economy and accuracy."[4] I am put in mind of the controversy surrounding the vernacular translation of the Bible from its original Hebrew and Greek, or of the dispute between Saints Jerome and Augustine over Jerome's Vulgate translation, the translation into Latin of the Hebrew and Greek Testaments. But it may, in part, be precisely his fidelity to initial principles that accounts for the relative critical neglect of or bemusement at this aspect of Hughes's work.

It is rather to his public role as a defender of the environment and the champion of the creativity of children than to his prominence as a literary figure that translation belongs, although he was not so much intent on displaying or exercising his skills as on introducing into our language, by whatever mean available (the most convenient being translation by himself), the work of significant writers of our time. He did not want these writings rendered palatably familiar by local writers, but sought to present them in their *otherness*, or, as he called it, rawness. Somewhat quixotically perhaps, even recklessly, Hughes was prepared to stake his reputation on what, at the time, amounted to a pioneering enterprise.

When he returned from the Spoleto Festival his interest in beginning a magazine devoted to poetry in translation had been fortified. Hughes did not envisage a literary magazine where literary works, especially poems, were decorously and tastefully displayed; what he had in mind was a kind of news-sheet or broadsheet, crammed with provisional versions, presented informally so as to encourage rapid scanning rather than critical assessment. The first *MPT* (1969) aimed to be such a publication and was issued in newspaper format, a well-known stratagem in those populist times. It is easy, then, to dismiss these ambitions of Hughes as characteristic of the 1960s, but his intention was to counter the preciosity of approach of contemporary literary magazines. He wanted *MPT* to be disposable, encouraging rapid perusal rather than relegation to bookshelves and library racks. Hence the format: flimsy stock and absence of scholarly or critical apparatus. Apart from consideration of costs, the purpose was to make room for as much primary material as possible, not to fill the space with commentary, which seemed of secondary importance. Even biographical information was minimalized, although Hughes recognized that translators maybe could do with some exposure, since their role typically received so little recognition.

What first alerted Hughes to the larger world of literature was his encounter, in the mid-1960s, with poetry from Eastern Europe, written by poets somewhat senior to himself. The Penguin "Modern European Poets" series was publishing lucidly translated poetry in inexpensive, conveniently slim collections. The general editor was the poet and critic A. Alvarez, who, in his Penguin anthology, *The New Poetry* (1962), gave pride of place to Ted Hughes's own early work.[5] The brevity encouraged by the format encouraged Hughes and myself to proceed with *MPT*, on the perhaps naïve assumption that if there were such striking writers with translators already in place, there must be more of them of comparable merit. The early Penguin collections included selections of Holub (Czechoslovakia, 1967), Herbert (Poland, 1968), Popa (Yugoslavia, 1969), Amichai (Israel 1969), Weöres and Juhász (Hungary, 1970), and Rózewicz (Poland, 1976). Some of these volumes were updated reprints of earlier small-press publications, which were later reprinted and augmented by these presses. Those most active in the UK in this pioneering effort to increase the range of poetry offered were initially Carcanet and Anvil, but Hughes persuaded his own publishers, Faber, to publish selections of Holub and Amichai, although this was somewhat later. Faber was disinclined to respond, on what Hughes judged an appropriate scale, to his enthusiasm for works by foreign poets he felt should be published in English translation. Bulk, in a way, is what Hughes was after; hence the need, as he saw it, for a periodical which would promote this poetry. Pilinzsky was published by Carcanet in the UK and Persea Books in the US, but his work did not appear in the Penguin series referred to above. Hughes's role, behind the scenes, was crucial and, of course, crucial in the founding of *MPT*.

Hughes's role was also central to the establishment of the International Poetry Festival. The first of these, in 1976, directed by Ted Hughes himself (and Patrick Garland), featured several American poets but, from the above list, Amichai only. Among the other poets reading, however, were the German Hans Magnus Enzensberger and the Austrian Ingeborg Bachmann, both already published in the UK, Enzensberger's work having been translated by one of the most active poet-translators, Michael Hamburger. With Christopher Middleton, Hamburger introduced readers to virtually the entire range of German poets of the postwar era, from both East and West Germany. The second Poetry International, in 1968, included Holub, Popa, and Pilinszky, and the third, in 1970, included Weöres from Hungary, and Amichai from Israel. Rózewicz and Amichai also read at the Fourth Poetry International in 1971.

We felt their poetry to be translatable, provided relatively few liberties were taken, translators confining themselves to translating the words on the page, rather than interpolating or projecting their fantasies and impressions. We came to the provisional conclusion that the writers of this generation had developed a universal language, hardly requiring the active intervention or special attention of interpreters or translators. This was explicable in terms of historical circumstances rather than naïvety about the translation process, arguably being a product of postwar idealism, or expressive of a rather last-ditch hope that people were capable of finding the means of communicating with one another, transcending language and cultural differences.

The belief in a universal desire for cultural inter-traffic was a matter of faith. but also substantiated by some influential scholarly texts, especially by Walter Benjamin's essay-introduction, "The Task of the Translator", to his own translation into German of poems by Baudelaire. This essay, re-published in English translation in the journal *Delos*, by the National Translation Center at the University of Texas, Austin, which had awarded our magazine a grant in its early stages, advanced the notion that the translation of a text pre-supposed a shadowy presence, located somewhere between source and target texts. Benjamin focused on Martin Buber's and Franz Rosenzweig's "foreignizing" translation of the Bible, the most significant one since Luther's. This land-mark essay was certainly read by Hughes. Indeed, Benjamin's thinking seems to underlie many of Hughes's assumptions about and comments on translation, notably in his Introduction to the London Poetry International programme, also used in our journal's publicity material, which included reference to Buber's "universal language". This statement may now seem optimistic, certainly polemical, a kind of fanfare for the "poetry games". In the forefront of Hughes's mind, however, was a serious and controversial notion: the "translatability" of the poetry.

Like Benjamin, Hughes posited an intermediate language, an *ur-sprache*, to which both source and target texts related. In this connection, one should cast one's mind back to that earlier period, characterized by insularism and a suspicion about or even hostility towards "foreignness", a time when it was possible for Larkin to remark that it would be fine to visit China provided one could be back in time for tea. Hughes's idea and, even more, the international readings, drew hostile fire from influential literary figures, Larkin amongst them, urging all the foreign poets to "go home" rather than lend themselves to so vulgar a "showbiz" event. Larkin had a point, since it was tactically difficult at that time for Hughes and other activists to stop this initiative from being co-opted by the public-relations industry. Hughes may have viewed the danger of vulgarization or reduction as less lethal than that of over-refinement, rendering poetry irrelevant to the concerns of most people. If – at least in recent times, in the English-language tradition – poetry is on the way to becoming irrelevant, the belief or hope in those days was that this development was not inevitable and that there was an argument to be made for poetry receiving a share of public funding.

This belief or hope was boosted by an increased awareness of the role of poetry in post-Stalin Russia, the relevance of poets, especially such as those mentioned, belonging to the first postwar Eastern European generation. For one thing, poetry in the declining years of the Soviet Union was becoming again a popular medium, with people like Yevtushenko filling sports stadiums with their readings. Boris Slutsky, a fine Soviet, war-era poet, had even written a poem entitled "Physicists and Lyricists", which placed poetry at the centre of the liberalization or modernizing process or tendency among the scientific as well as artistic intelligentsia. That there was a limit to the boldness of the likes of Yevtushenko, whose role was ambivalent, was not, at least in the West, recognized until somewhat later and then only by specialists. Poets in Eastern Europe and the Soviet Union itself were not regarded as detached from historical currents; on the contrary, they were often seen as being in the vanguard, as they had been much earlier, at the time of the October Revolution, in quite different historical circumstances. Yevtushenko and others, indeed, appeared on the scene in the guise of "Romantic Revolutionaries", and there was talk of restoring so-called Leninist norms, harking back to origins which, with scant historical justification, were regarded as having been violated by the undemocratic regime of Lenin and his successors. This tendency appealed to many in the West and its significance was somewhat overrated by those hoping for changes, maybe even a rejection by the Soviet Union of its imperialistic ambitions.

While it can be argued that observers and commentators in the West were deluding themselves, it should be borne in mind that this applied also to writers in the Soviet sphere of influence, in post-Stalin Europe, if it be not invidious to call such modest hopes or aspirations towards independence delusory at the time. A. Alvarez was in the forefront, with a series of broadcasts on artists and intellectuals in Communist countries, later published by Penguin.[6] Alvarez referred, in some detail, to these matters, via interviews with significant writers; he was also, as noted, in charge of "Penguin Modern European Poets", which posited a reunited Europe, drawing attention to the importance of poetry translation in our time. His critical book contextualized the significance in Eastern Europe of the role of writers, especially poets, marginalized in the UK – although less so in the (often campus-based) Vietnam War-"protest" period in the USA. This realization prompted some rethinking of the role of language in national self-identification, especially relevant when considering the countries of Eastern Europe, for so long invisible or inaudible in the Austro-Hungarian, and Soviet empires.

Hughes contributed an essay to a special issue of *Modern Poetry in Translation* (1972), in which he looks back on this period and tries to identify forces and trends. He refers to several factors: "the mass epidemic of infatuation with hallucinogenic drugs, the sudden opening to all of the worlds of Eastern mystical practice and doctrine, particularly of various forms of Buddhism, the mass craze of Hippie ideology, the revolt of the young, the Pop music of the Beatles and their generation, the Walpurgisnacht of new psychotherapies." He was not being judgmental about a period which had at least managed to engage and harness the energy and idealism of the young. Hughes had, after all, himself been interested in Buddhist writings, especially, as we have seen, when he was working on an oratorio for a proposed stage version of *The Tibetan Book of the Dead* and he had sampled the "new psychotherapies" as a result of his collaboration with Peter Brook's experimental theatre workshop in Paris.

He was, in short, more a creature of his time than is often recognized, his brainchild *MPT* being a product of this same time, in its inclusiveness and anti-élitism. Ted Hughes's career is, to some extent, identifiable with an upsurge that was to change the composition of England's intellectual élite, even if he himself was a product of Cambridge, one of the strongholds of that élite, having been admitted by virtue of intellectual promise rather than social connections. At my request, he wrote an essay-editorial, at a time when *MPT* was undergoing one of its periodic metamorphoses and was to re-emerge as an annual survey, published by Carcanet in the UK and Persea Books in the USA.[7] He attempted to put the enterprise of poetry translation in postwar Britain into its historical perspective. I shall not attempt to summarize or analyse a text which embodies a plethora of intuitions and was primarily intended to function as a promotional boost for a journal which had managed to get translated poetry taken as a legitimate form of literary endeavour.

There was probably a keener awareness of the danger of greater-language-chauvinism in America than in England, which perhaps accounts in part for Hughes's scheme for a poetry magazine devoted to the presentation of poetry in translation meeting with so positive a response in the USA.

Hughes was drawn to the lively translation scene in the States, which he felt was more genuinely responsive to radical or experimental projects than was England, still largely dominated by a social establishment.

So, in a world in which other poetries were becoming visible and being made accessible by translators who seemed to have been waiting for the opportunity to render the rest of us this service, Hughes saw little to get in the way, provided, of course, translators did not forefront themselves. Underpinning this conviction was a belief in the universal nature of human sensibility, rendering translation not only possible but necessary.

Notes

Introduction
pp.7–14

1. Programme, Poetry International, Arts Council of Great Britain, 1967.
2. Recordings of two talks were made available as LPs by the BBC in 1971: "Learning to Think" (1961) and "Capturing Animals" (1963). The talks were published in part in Hughes, Ted. *Poetry in the Making.* London: Faber, 1967, and as *Poetry Is.* New York: Doubleday, 1970.
3. See, for example, *A Dancer to God: Tributes to T.S. Eliot.* London: Faber, 1992; New York: Farrar, Straus & Giroux, 1993; Hughes, Ted. *Winter Pollen: Occasional Prose.* London: Faber, 1994; New York: Picador, 1995.
4. *Shakespeare and the Goddess of Complete Being.* London: Faber, 1992; New York: Farrar, Straus & Giroux, 1992 (corrected and expanded edition). Faber paperback edition (also corrected and expanded), 1993.
5. *A Choice of Emily Dickinson's Verse*, selected and with an introduction by Ted Hughes. London: Faber, 1968; *Keith Douglas: The Complete Poems*, edited with a new preface by Desmond Graham; introduction by Ted Hughes. Oxford: Oxford University Press, 1998.
6. *A Choice of Shakespeare's Verse*, selected with an introduction by Ted Hughes. London: Faber, 1971.
7. *Modern Poetry in Translation*, no.3, Spring 1967.
8. Eliot, T.S. *Collected Essays.* London: Faber, 1932, p.59.
9. Havel, Vaclav, *Open Letters: Selected Writings, 1965-1990.* New York: Vintage, 1992.
10. *Modern Poetry in Translation Yearbook*, 1983. The first and only volume in an intended series of annual collections, to replace the quarterly magazine.
11. Yates, Frances A. *The Art of Memory.* London: Routledge and Kegan Paul, 1966.
12. *The Five Books of Moses*, translated by Everett Fox. New York: Schocken, 1995.
13. Pound, Ezra. *Literary Essays of Ezra Pound.* New York: New Directions, 1968.
14. Introduction to Amichai, Yehuda. *Amen.* New York: Harper & Row, 1977; Oxford: Oxford University Press, 1979.
15. 'Postscript to János Csokits's Note' in Weissbort, Daniel, ed. *Translating Poetry: The Double Labyrinth.* Iowa City: University of Iowa Press; London: Macmillan, 1989.
16. Ted Hughes archive, Emory University, Atlanta. See also Chapter III.

I

Modern Poetry in Translation

pp.15-25

1. Introduction, *Collected Poems of Vasko Popa*. London: Anvil, 1978.
2. Pilinszky, János. *János Pilinszky: Selected Poems*, translated by Ted Hughes and János Csokits. Manchester: Carcanet, 1977; New York: Persea Books, 1977; reissued as *The Desert of Love*, London: Anvil, 1989.
3. See Introduction, note 15.
4. See note 2, above.
5. In Weissbort, Daniel, ed. *Translating Poetry*, see note 3 above.
6. Quoted in Ted Hughes, Introduction to *The Desert of Love*, see note 2, above.
7. See note 2, above.
8. Introduction to *Amen*, New York: Harper & Row, 1977; Oxford: Oxford University Press, 1978.
9. Letter to Amichai, Emory University.
10. *Ibid.*
11. See Lawrence Venuti, *The Translator's Invisibility*. London: Routledge, 2006.
12. W.H.I. Bleek and L.C. Lloyd, *Specimens of Bushman Folklore*. London: George Allen, 1911. The complete text is available online at http://www.archive.org/stream/specimensofbushm00bleeuoft/specimensofbushm00bleeuoft_djvu.txt
13. See Introduction, note 10.
14. Ramanujan, A.K. *Speaking of Siva*. London: Penguin Books, 1973.
15. Benjamin, Walter. "The Task of the Translator", in *Illuminations*, London: Fontana, 1992, available online at http://site.ebrary.com/lib/uoh/Doc?id=10100314&ppg=27
16. *The Five Books of Moses*, see Introduction, note 12.
17. *New Republic*, 4 August 1941; reprinted in *Vladimir Nabokov: Lectures on Russian Literature*, New York: Harcourt Brace Jovanovich, 1981; London, Weidenfeld and Nicolson, 1982.
18. Lermontov, Mikhail. *A Hero of Our Time*. Oxford: Oxford University Press, 1992. Ibid.
20. First published in *Partisan Review*, no. XXII, 1955.

II
Yehuda Amichai: The Authenticity of Self-Translation
pp.26–38

1. *Yehuda Amichai: Selected Poems*, translated by Assia Gutmann, London: Cape Goliard, 1968; Amichai, Yehuda. *Amen*, translated by the author and Ted Hughes; with an introduction by Ted Hughes. Oxford; New York: Oxford University Press, 1978. Amichai, Yehuda. *Time*, translated by the author with Ted Hughes. Oxford; New York: Oxford University Press, 1979.
2. *Yehuda Amichai: Selected Poems*, edited by Ted Hughes and Daniel Weissbort. London: Faber, 2000.
3. Robert Alter. "The Untranslatable Amichai", *Modern Hebrew Literature*, no.13, 1994.
4. Hughes-Amichai correspondence, Emory University.
5. Letter, *c.*1970, Emory University.
6. Letter, 8 December, 1985, Emory University.
7. See Chapter I, note 8.
8. *Open Closed Open: The Selected Poetry of Yehuda Amichai*, edited and newly translated by Chana Bloch and Stephen Mitchell. London:Viking, 1987.
9. Letter, 17 July 1973, Emory University.
10. Letter, 1 July 1977, Emory University.
11. Letter, 14 May 1983, Emory University.
12. Letter, *c.*1970, Emory University.
13. Letter, November 1975, Emory University.
14. Burnshaw, Stanley, ed. *The Poem Itself*. New York: Holt, Rinehart and Winston, 1960.
15. See note 2, above.
16. Roberts, Neil. *Ted Hughes: A Literary Life*. London: Palgrave Macmillan, 2006.

III
János Pilinsky: The Troubled Mechanic
pp.39–52

1. Pilinszky, János. *Conversations with Sheryl Sutton: The Novel of a Dialogue*, Riverdale NY: Sheep Meadow Press, 1992.
2. Nemes Nagy, Ágnes, "Janos Pilinszky: A Very Different Poet", *Hungarian Quarterly 22*, no.84, Winter 1981.
3. See Chapter I, note 4.
4. Juhász, Ferenc. *The Boy Changed into a Stag: Selected Poems, 1949-67*, Edited and translated by Kenneth McRobbie and Ilona Duczynska. Toronto: Oxford University Press, 1970.
5. Koncz, Lajos. "Ted Hughes and János Pilinszky", *Hungarian Quarterly*, vol. XII, no.171, Autumn 2007.
6. See Introduction, note 15.
7. Lowell, Robert. *Imitations*. London: Faber 1962.
8. See Introduction, note 15.
9. See Chapter I, note 2.
10. BBC World Service, 18 September 1976.
11. See Chapter I, note 2.

IV
European Poets, Past and Present
pp.53-57

1. See Weissbort, Daniel, ed. *Ted Hughes: Selected Translations*. London: Faber 2006.
2. *Ibid.*
3. *Ibid.*
4. Letter, Emory University.
5. *Modern Poetry in Translation*, no.16, Special French issue, 1973.
6. Letter, Emory University.

V
Ovid's *Metamorphoses*: To Tell a Story
pp.58-62

1. Miller, Frank Justus. *Ovid: Metamorphoses, Books I-VIII*, London: Heinemann; Cambridge MA: Harvard University Press, 1957.
2. Rouse, W.H.D., ed. *Shakespeare's Ovid: being Arthur Golding's translation of the Metamorphoses*. London: De La More Press, 1904; available online at http://www.elizabethanauthors.com/ovid00.htm
3. Hofmann, Michael and Lasdun, James, eds. *After Ovid: New Metamorphoses*. London: Faber, 1994.
4. Hughes, Ted. *Tales from Ovid: Twenty-four Passages from the Metamorphoses*. London: Faber; New York: Farrar Straus and Giroux, 1997.
5. Hughes, Ted. *Shakespeare and the Goddess of Complete Being*. London: Faber, 1992.
6. See Chapter 4, note 1.
7. Pound, Ezra. *Literary Essays*. New York: New Directions, 1968.
8. Hill, D.E. *Ovid: Metamorphoses I-IV*, 1985; *Ovid: Metamorphoses, Book I*. Mundelein, Ill: Bolchazy-Carducci Publishers, 1953.
9. Nims, John Frederick, ed. *Ovid's Metamorphoses: The Arthur Golding Translation 1567*. Philadelphia: Paul Dry Books, 2000.
10. See note 4, above.

VI
Ferenc Juhász : History of a Translation
pp.63-66

1. See Chapter III, note 4.
2. *Sandor Weöres, Ferenc Juhász: Selected Poems*. Harmondsworth: Penguin, 1970.
3. The complete Hughes text of the poem, including some corrections, is reprinted in *Looking Eastward, Modern Poetry in Translation*, new series, no.21, 2003.

VII

Phèdre, The Oresteia: Metre and Grandiloquence
pp.67–76

1. Racine, Jean, *Phaedra*, translated by Robert Lowell. London: Faber, 1963; and see Lowell, Robert. *Collected Prose.* New York: Farrar Straus and Giroux, 1987
2. *The Oresteia of Aeschylus*, translated by Robert Lowell, London: Faber, 1979.
3. Harrison, Tony. *Phaedra Britannica.* London: Rex Collings, 1975.
4. *The Oresteia*, in a version by Ted Hughes. London: Faber, 1999.
5. See note 2, above.
6. Grene, Richard and Lattimore, Richmond, eds. *The Complete Greek Tragedies*, Vol.1, Chicago: University of Chicago Press, 1955.
7. Aeschylus. *Oresteia.* London: Duckworth, 2001.
8. Racine, Jean. *Iphigenia; Phaedra; Athaliah* translated and introduced by John Cairncross, Harmondsworth: Penguin, 1963.

VIII

The Tibetan Book of the Dead: An Oratorio
pp.78-85

1. Hughes, Ted, *Lupercal.* London: Faber 1960.
2. Evans-Wentz, W.Y., ed. *The Tibetan Book of the Dead or The After-Death Experiences on the Bardo Plane, according to Lama Kazi Dawa-Samdup's English Rendering.* London: Oxford University Press, 3rd edition, 1957.
3. 'Regenerations', review of Mircea Eliade's *Shamanism, The Listener,* 29 October 1964, reprinted in Hughes, Ted. *Winter Pollen.* London: Faber, 1994.
4. Premiere at the London Coliseum, 1974; broadcast on BBC Radio 3, 21 March 1974.
5. Hughes, Ted. *Remains of Elmet: A Pennine Sequence.* London: Faber, 1979.
6. Hughes, Ted. *Wodwo.* London: Faber, 1967.
7. Interview, Adelaide Festival, March 1976, transcribed by Ann Skea: online at http://annskea.com/ABC2AF.htm
8. Eliade, Mircea. *Shamanism: Archaic Techniques of Ecstasy*, translated from the French by Willard R. Trask. Princeton, NJ: Princeton University Press, 1964.
9. Euripides. *Alcestis*, in a new version by Ted Hughes. London: Faber, 1999. Premiere at the Viaduct Theatre, Halifax, September 1999.
10. Myers, Lucas. *An Essential Self: Ted Hughes and Sylvia Plath.* Nottingham: Richard Hollis/Five Leaves, 2011.
11. Cox, C.B., Dyson, A.E., eds. *Black Papers on Education.* London: HarperCollins, 1971.

IX

Peter Brook: Drama as Paradigm

pp.86–100

1. Hardy, Thomas. *Late Lyrics and Earlier: With Many Other Verses*. London: Macmillan, 1922.
2. Hughes, Ted. *Orghast*. London: Methuen 1972.
3. Eliot, T. S. *Selected Essays 1917-1932*. London: Faber, 1932
4. Source uncertain, but see: Brook, Peter. *The Shifting Point: Forty Years of Theatrical Exploration, 1946-1987*. London: Methuen, 1988; Williams, David, ed. *Peter Brook: A Theatrical Casebook*, London: Methuen, 1992; Hunt, Albert and Reeves, Geoffrey. *Peter Brook*. Cambridge: Cambridge University Press, 1995
5. Source uncertain. See note 4, above.
5. Turner was a BBC radio producer.
7. Introduction, Seneca's *Oedipus*, adapted by Ted Hughes. London: Faber, 1969.
8. *Ibid.*
9. Interview, Adelaide Festival, March 1976,transcribed by Ann Skea: online at http://www.zeta.org.au/~annskea/ABC2AF.htm
10. Alexander Neville (1544-1614). *Seneca: His Tenne Tragedies*, translated into English in 1581 by Jasper Heywood; Alexander Neville; John Studley et al. Manchester: Charles E.Simms & Co., 1887. Online at http://www.elizabethanauthors.com/ovid00.htm10.
11. See note 7, above.
12. The Ted Hughes Collection at the University of Liverpool includes drafts of the play, proofs and correspondence relating to the translation and production.
13. Source uncertain. See note 4, above.
14. Lorca, Federico García, *In Search of Duende*. New York: New Directions, 1998.

X

Orghast: The Continuing Search for a Universal Language

pp.101–105

1. "The Task of the Translator", an introduction to the translation of Baudelaire's *Tableaux Parisiens*, in Venuti, Lawrence, *Translation Studies Reader*, London: Routledge, 1999. Available online at http://site.ebrary.com/lib/uoh/Doc?id=10100314&ppg=27
2. Grotowski, Jerzy. *Towards a Poor Theatre*, edited by Eugenio Barba, with a preface by Peter Brook. London: Methuen, 1969.
3. Smith, A.C.H. *Orghast at Persepolis*. London: Eyre Methuen, 1972.
4. Bentley, Paul. *The Poetry of Ted Hughes: Language, Illusion and Beyond*. Harlow: Longman 1998.
5. See note 3, above.
6. "Orghast", *Times Literary Supplement*, 1 October 1971.
7. Attar, Farid al-Din. *The Conference of the Birds*, edited and translated by Afkham Darbandi and Dick Davis. Harmondsworth: Penguin, 1984.

XI

The Last Translation: Pushkin's *The Prophet*
pp.106–111

1. See Weissbort, Daniel, ed. *Ted Hughes: Selected Translations*, London: Faber 2006, Appendix 15.

XII

Conclusion
pp.112–120

1. Steiner, George. *After Babel: Aspects of Language and Translation*. London: Oxford University Press, 1975.
2. See Chapter II, note 14.
3. Pushkin, Aleksandr Sergeevich. *Eugene Onegin*, translated from the Russian, with a commentary, by Vladimir Nabokov. London: Routledge & Kegan Paul, 1964.
4. See Chapter I, note 2.
5. *The New Poetry*, an anthology selected and introduced by A. Alvarez. Harmondsworth: Penguin, 1962 and Alvarez. A. *Under Pressure: The Writer in Society: Eastern Europe and the USA*. Baltimore MD: Penguin, 1965.
6. Penguin Modern European Poets:
   Zbigniew Herbert: Selected Poems, translated by Czesław Miłosz and Peter Dale Scott, with an introduction by A. Alvarez, 1968;
   Vasco Popa, translated by Anne Pennington, 1969;
   Yehuda Amichai: Selected Poems, translated by Assia Gutman and Harold Schimmel with the collaboration of Ted Hughes, 1969;
   Sándor Weöres and Ferenc Juhász, translated by Edwin Morgan and David Wevill, 1970;
   Tadeusz Rózewicz: Selected Poems, translated with an introduction by Adam Czerniawski, 1976;
   Miroslav Holub; Selected Poems, translated by Ian Milner and George Theiner with an introduction by A. Alvarez, 1977.
7. Alvarez, A. *Under Pressure: The Writer in Society: Eastern Europe and the USA*. Baltimore, MD: Penguin, 1965.

Acknowledgments

This book was prepared for the conference "Ted Hughes: From Cambridge to 'Collected'" at Pembroke College, Cambridge, September 2010.

The publisher thanks Carol Hughes, Daniel Huws, Valentina Polukhina and Ann Skea for their help, and is grateful to Hana Amichai for permission to publish letters and translations of her late husband.

Unpublished translations and letters are from typescripts or manuscripts, mostly in the Ted Hughes archive in Special Collections at Emory University, Atlanta, USA, and also in the Ted Hughes Collection at Liverpool University. They are published here by kind permission of the Estate of Ted Hughes.

Bibliographical details of published translations are given in the Notes. Extracts from some translations are republished from *Ted Hughes: Selected Translations* (London: Faber and Faber, 2006), edited by Daniel Weissbort.

Also published
by Richard Hollis and Five Leaves

An Essential Self:
Ted Hughes and Sylvia Plath
A memoir by Lucas Myers

——

Memories of Ted Hughes 1952–1963
Daniel Huws

——

Susan Alliston
Poems and Journals 1960–1969
Introduction by Ted Hughes